IN A DUSTY MIRROR

IN A DUSTY MIRROR

RHYME, RHYTHM AND REMINISCENCE

JOHN BELCHER

First published in 2014 by:
John Belcher

ISBN:978-0-9930335-0-6

Printed and bound in Great Britain by:
Book Printing UK, Remus House, Coltsfoot Drive, Woodston,
Peterborough PE2 9BF

1 1 0605014 3

This book is dedicated to my daughter, Ruth.

Foreword

Having been involved in poetry publishing for over twenty five years, I have read, edited and published many poetry collections, but this one is different.

In all those years I have not come across another volume like this eclectic pot-pourri of Edward Lear style humorous nonsense poems, beautifully sad love poems and autobiographical accounts of the author's war time childhood, travels and astonishing adventures in the Sudan and other parts of Africa.

Many of the pages are illustrated with his own skilful pen-and-ink drawings.

Intriguing, interesting, instructive – I recommend it.

Roger Hoult.
Editor – Salopeot Magazine (The Salopian Poetry Society).

Introduction

This book started as an anthology of poetry written over the years since I was eighteen, previous work, sadly, having been lost. But threading its way through the poems is a discontinuous series of memoirs dating from before World War Two. It is not intended to be an autobiography but, in order to record each event accurately, sometimes it has been necessary to be in the picture myself.

There is, at the time of writing, a generation around, God bless 'em, who can remember life in the early days of this narrative, a tough generation brought up on wartime rations with freedom to roam and play without inhibitions. Obesity was very rare in those days. Perhaps some passages in this book will rekindle nostalgic memories of your own, as they have done for me while writing. It is hoped that younger generations will get a better insight into life as it was in those days.

Having travelled extensively in Africa, I could have written about such places as the Valley of the Kings, Table Mountain or Victoria Falls but plenty has already been written and documented about those fantastic places and, politics permitting, they are relatively easy to visit. Find me a package tour that will take me across the vast volcanic crater of Jebel Marra in western Sudan, mix with villagers on the triple border of Sudan, Kenya and Uganda or even take me for a ride on the Banana Express, and I will struggle to think of more remote and exciting places.

Although primarily intended for an adult readership, some of the poems in this book are obviously written with children in mind. You may well ask why they are included. Is there a poetry-lover who is not enamoured by the delightful nonsense of Edward Lear, Lewis Carroll and others? You have your answer!

In a Dusty Mirror

The room was damp and rather cold,
Grey cobwebs hung in corners.
The old distemper on the walls
Had tales to tell of mourners.
Damp patches rising from the ground
Depicted tales so dreary,
A traveller I, nowhere to stay,
Happed on this room so eerie.

The murm'ring wind, the creaking boards
Redolent of human voice,
I wished for somewhere else to sleep
But, broke, I had no choice.
I'd travelled far that very day
With mind and body shattered,
At least there was a roof up there;
That's all that really mattered.

A dusty mirror on the wall
Devoid of information,
I thought I saw an image there,
Perhaps hallucination,
And as my jaded mind gave way
To dreams and such illusion
The image murmured through the dust
Compounding my confusion.

"You're looking at a man," it said,
"A man who never was.
I wear size ten in shoes just like
My elder brother does,
An engineer or draughtsman, I,
Who went to tech' or grammar,
An artist or a referee
Or auctioneer with hammer,

A fam'ly man, an honest man,
A man who likes a game,
A godly man, hard-working man
Or rogue, it's all the same.
I'm all these things
And yet I'm not, if I'm to be believed;
My father died beside The Somme
Before I was conceived."

The Goldfish and the Salmon

Said the goldfish to the salmon
"How I envy you your lot;
You've the freedom of the river
While I'm stuck in this glass pot.
You can dance about in waterfalls
Like poetry in motion
And, when you've had enough of that,
You'll swim down to the ocean."

"Ah! But!," the salmon said in haste,
"You're safe and sound in here;
While I am dodging fishing lines
You've nothing left to fear.
There's awful danger waiting there
And threats on ev'ry fin;
If I don't keep my wits alert
I'll end up in a tin."

And so the goldfish, satisfied,
Resumed her discoid motion
And quite forgot she once aspired
To swim down to the ocean,
But one day, when the fam'ly cat
Was feeling pangs of hunger,
He took a swipe into the bowl;
The goldfish was no longer.

"You naughty cat," the lady said,
"You really should have waited,
Look what the Master's caught for you
On hook and line well baited."
You've guessed the rest, of course,
There is no need to tell the story
How Sam and Goldie ended up
Both fin in fin in Glory.

Amy

She lived in Kings Heath
With a wire in her teeth
'Cause her dentals were apt to protrude.
I now say it with shame
Of poor Amy, her name,
That the boys often said something rude.

She was seven years old
And was in the same fold
As we sat day by day in our school.
She was one of those girls
With straight hair and no curls
That would pass without note, as a rule.

Then one terrible night
There was such a dog-fight
Overhead – the whole world helter-skelter.
Bombs were falling galore
As we crouched on the floor
Of the cellar which served as a shelter.

The morning dawned cool
And we all went to school,
All, that is, bar one, her desk bare.
The teacher was grim
And we all sang a hymn
And then put on our gas masks with care.

There were many more nights
When we blacked out our lights
And hoped we would live till the morning,
But, at seven years old,
Here's to Amy the bold.
Will the world ever heed her dread warning?

Ode to the Person who nicked our Wheelybin

We hope you will have lots of fun,
Now that your recycling is done,
Putting all your gooey trash,
Marmalade and ciggy ash,
Hole-ey socks and poo-ey naps
In the bin that once, perhaps,
Filled us with ecstatic joy
To all our leisure time employ
Throwing stuff no longer needed
In the bin that now we've ceded
To a silent, faceless foe.
Now it's nicked so now you know!

P.S.   We thought of writing quite a curse
        But what's the use, it could be worse.

Requiem to the bin:
       You were such a lovely wheely;
       Nought with you could 'ere compare,
       Black below with wheels so gorgeous,
       Red on top like Fergie's hair.
       How we miss you in the mornin'
       When the dew lay on your lid
       And at even, night was born in
       Till in shadows you were hid.

Early Memories

The Austin Seven jingled along at somewhere near its maximum speed of forty-five to fifty miles an hour. They always jingled, those Austin Sevens! There was a starting handle permanently fitted to the front which had a brass sleeve to stop you getting blisters. That jingled! Inside, there was a chromium-plated bell-shaped cover at the bottom of the gear lever, that also jingled!

It was loaded, a man and a woman in the front, a teenage girl, her small brother and a dog in the back. On the retractable outside carrier was a large trunk containing camping equipment. The leather seats gave out a familiar, comforting aroma.

We were on our way to Southsea a couple of years before World War Two started. This was to be our last holiday for a long time. For me, it was the first holiday I can remember. My father, a tailor, had made the tent himself, complete with fly-sheet and some pitch-paper to act as a ground sheet.

The campsite was a green rectangle with a standpipe tap in one corner and a toilet block in another. My father had made a canvas bucket which he proceeded to half fill with water and then swing it round in circles so that, even when it was upside down, the water did not fall out. My first lesson in centrifugal force!

When we had pumped up the lorry inner tube, which was to act as a buoyancy aid when in the sea, a boy about a year older than me came over and suggested that I "steck a pen en it". This shocked me on two fronts, for a start I had never before come across anyone with a desire to deliberately spoil a useful object and, not having been exposed to any other accents except the "Brummie" of my mother and the London of my father, I questioned whether a 'pen' was really the best tool for the job.

My memory of time spent on the beach has been diluted by many similar experiences in later life but memory of the paddle-steamer to the Isle of Wight will never fade. My father took me to an observation panel where we saw the mighty cranks, piston rods and connecting rods rhythmically turning the shaft that drove the paddle wheels. They reminded me of giant bicycle cranks. It always annoys me now when I see signs pointing 'To the Steamers', knowing that the only steam on board will be created by the process of making tea.

One day we went to a display of the might of the Royal Navy. We watched un-armed torpedoes launched across the bay and we went in a submarine. I was bought a little stuffed sailor and then we got lost in the crowd, I was with my father, and my sister with our mother. After a few minutes of apprehension, a message on the loudspeaker system reunited us. We had been standing very near to each other all the time.

On the way home, we stopped for a break and the dog rolled in some manure. My father said, not too seriously I now think, that we would have to leave him there – tears! Eventually, he was rubbed with a towel and allowed access to the tiny car. The pleasant smell of the car's leather interior was no longer noticeable.

Once Bitten

When I was at school, a teacher came,
I won't give away her maiden name,
She said, "I want you all to frame
A poem in this lesson."

Well, I felt inspired so my ink just flowed
As I wrote about a voice from a cloud
And finished before the time allowed –
The forty-minute session.

The paper marked, she said "Pooh – pooh,
I don't believe this came from you.
You've memorised the whole thing through.
You ought to get detention."

She gave the prize to a boy who wrote
A two-line ditty I will not quote,
About a dog with a sandy coat,
But he wrote with good intention.

The papers all went in the bin,
An act that really was a sin
'Cause I can't remember what was in
The poem that I'd written.

The odd thing is, I remember now –
The doggy ditty's survived somehow –
I learnt a lot that day, and now
I'm not so easily bitten.

The War Years

Two tailoresses assisted my father in his workshop attached to our house. One of them, Mrs Lilly, used to look down my throat every morning and tell me what I had had for breakfast. She was always right. I did not suspect at the time that she may have had an accomplice.

One day my father was repairing a leaky skylight on the workshop roof. He had taken out the frame, removed the glass and left the skeletal structure leaning up against the end of the building. Ah, a ladder! I climbed to the top and peered along the roof. My horrified father glared back from his perch on a step-ladder inside, his head sticking out of the hole. Fetching my mother, they both stood waiting to catch me at the bottom of the 'ladder'. I wondered what the fuss was all about and climbed down unscathed.

Before the demands of education destroyed my happy routine I almost lived in that workshop. Offcuts of cloth were put in hessian sacks and stored under a workbench. This was my den; I arranged them into 'walls' and wallpapered the inside. Periodically a man would come and take them all away, thus my first experience of recycling was not a happy one.

When I grew tall enough to hang with one hand from the top of a sewing machine and reach the treadle with my feet, I used to make iron-holders for use with a large tailors' iron. It was made of solid iron (hence the name) and the handle would get very hot, so about seven thicknesses of cloth were sewn together into a pad to protect his hand. One day my left index finger, still very small, went under the foot and the needle pierced straight through it. Help quickly came and the flywheel was turned back to restore my freedom.

At this time there was a lot of adult talk about a guy called Hitler. I don't remember seeing The Wizard of Oz but each time I heard the name Hitler, a mental image of a tin man came to mind. In the days before television, having mental images of voices on the radio was the norm. I can only assume that the Tin

Man had scared me and, when I gathered that Hitler was a scary person, it must be the same man.

When the war started, my father, who had served in the First World War and was by then of an age when his services were no longer needed, gave up his business and took a job as a tailoring instructor at a hospital for people with learning difficulties. Having sold the Austin Seven we moved house so that he could be near his work. Every day he would come home and entertain us with a commentary of the humorous antics that had gone on in the day. I gather that little tailoring was accomplished but it seemed that his brief was more one of occupational therapy than actually producing clothes. In his spare time he made suits and costumes for other members of staff to supplement his wage of about £4.00 per week.

The inmates were known in our household as 'the chaps'. Before my father's time they had rarely been allowed outside the boundaries of the institution, but he persuaded the powers that be, namely the Super', the Matron and I'm not sure who else, to introduce some innovations. A parole system was established for those capable of conducting themselves wisely in the outside world. They were issued with passes, some pocket money (at first from my father's pocket), and given a time to be back. Failure on the latter point could lead to parole being withdrawn.

On Sundays he used to invite a couple of 'chaps' home for lunch on a rota basis. My parents formed the opinion that not all the chaps were all that slow at learning; some were the victims of a society unable to make up its mind what to do with people who failed to fit in with its criteria.

At night the staff worked a fire-watching rota, usually a fairly easy job except that you had to be awake all night and then work next day. One night three staff members were standing outside the blast wall of the games room when a stray bomb killed them all. Fortunately my father was not on duty that night. Maybe that was the same night I was sleeping with our white cat, 'Puffy', purring away on my pillow when I dreamt a small red light, like a lighted cigarette, was coming toward me out of the darkness. Just as it approached my face there was a mighty big boom and we were nearly thrown out of the bed.

On the morning after a raid we children used to search around for pieces of shrapnel and incendiary bomb tails and line up these trophies on our window sills. We accepted these harsh years as just life. It was our parents who did the worrying.

We had bikes and I used to ride out with my parents to beauty-spots like the Lickey Hills at weekends. During the school holidays we played in the field behind the houses. At the outbreak of war a housing estate had just begun to be built but, with nobody to continue it, it was abandoned and became a wild playground for us. In keeping with the times, we dug underground dens and engaged in pitched battles with the Lindsworth gang who, bombed out from the inner city, had been allocated requisitioned houses, built but not occupied on another estate the other side of the field. We erected a zip-wire across the trees but our fun was terminated by a lady who objected to us zipping past her upstairs windows.

In the evenings we listened to radio programs like ITMA (It's that man again.), starring Tommy Handley and his retinue of zany callers; Mrs Mop, Colonel Chinstrap, Fumph, etc., each with their own catchphrase. How I'd like to see it re-written for television! There was a lot of good family comedy on the radio at that time. This phase of my life ended with the war, we moved again and another era began.

A Poet's Dream

He writes lots of poems, some happy, some sad.
Maybe some folks read them; they can't be too bad.
Perhaps when he's gone they will realise his worth
And place lovely flowers on his bit of earth.

A guide will show tourists the place he was born.
At Christie's they'll auction the cap he has worn.
Museum with relics – security high!
The school where he studied, his blue and white tie.

They may name an airport, a ship or a town,
Erect a memorial on some grassy down.
A new chosen subject now on Mastermind,
The life and the works of our poet you'll find.
On all the best quizzes again and again,
A question about him – your starter for ten.

Curriculum subjects will honour his name.
The culture of Britain will ne'er be the same.
On T.V. commercials you'll oft find a quote
Promoting their products with something he wrote.

But dreams have a habit of fading away
As sure as the night flees the coming of day,
For fame is as fickle as fickle can be,
There's no correlation with what ought to be.
So patience, dear poet, like Jude the Obscure,
Perhaps you will never write much to endure,
But just keep on writing, you never do know
What heart you may comfort by seeds that you sow.

Ouch! Where's the Sticking Plaster?

The health and safety factory man
Called at our place one day.
He said he'd come to check
That all the tools were put away
And were we wearing safety boots?
That's all he had to say.

But when he sent in his report
He said he'd come again
To see if there was anything endangering the men
And women too, for all must work
In circumstances safe.
He didn't want folks going home
With half a hand or face.

Were presses guarded, made foolproof?
Did we wear safety glasses?
Was there sufficient air about
To dispel nasty gasses?
Did we leave things just lying round
For folks to stub their toe?
For human safety's paramount.
That's what we all must know.

No doubt you are all wondering
What we folks manufacture.
Well, we are making cluster bombs.
Land mines we make much faster,
And hand grenades, and bayonets.
Ouch! Where's the sticking-plaster?

The Market Hall and its Clock

It stood at the top end of the Bull Ring, facing the cobbled street where rows of costermongers, with their barrows, lined the steep incline rising from St. Martin's Church. Inside, the Market Hall had stalls selling all kinds of goods. I cannot remember much about the 'respectable' stalls but I remember the 'junk' ones, something akin to the modern car boot sale. There were stalls selling old, wind-up gramophone motors. Now, what could you do with an old gramophone motor? Put it in an old gramophone, perhaps, or use it to drive some kind of working model? These sorts of things fascinated me, and still do.

The most memorable thing, however, was the clock. It was fixed to the wall half-way between the door and the end of the building. It appeared to be made entirely out of cast iron, although I'm sure there must have been some more delicate parts out of sight of my enquiring eyes. On the hour, figures would appear from doors, carrying large hammers which they would then proceed to bash onto bells, for the required number of times according to the time of day, after which, in silence, they would sedately return to their recondite positions. I always looked forward to the opportunity of watching this procedure.

One night, during an air-raid on the city, my mother was watching the fray from the dining-room window of our house, which stood on a rise about six miles from the town centre. An extra-large flash, followed by an extra-large 'boom', lit up the sky. Without any hesitation at all "That was the Market Hall", she said. How she knew, if she knew, I have never found out.

Next day, she took me to Town to do some shopping. We surveyed the damage from the previous night's raid, contents of shops strewn around on roads and pavements, and walls hanging dangerously at precarious angles. Oddly enough, life went on as usual, shoppers picking their way through the rubble to reach shops which had escaped the worst.

We went to the Market Hall. The shell of the building was there, minus the roof. We went inside. Climbing over piles of bricks and stone, we eventually saw it, its dismembered and broken parts protruding from piles of rubble. I cried, just as I do now when I recall that day!

The Clock

Small boy stood in the Market Hall,
Oblivious to the costers' call,
Awaiting sound that would enthral,
Impatient for the hour.
With bated breath he watched in awe,
Eleven fifty-nine, no more,
A whirring sound began to soar,
Then came the figures dour.

Through an open door they marched,
Hammers raised and back-bones arched,
Reached the bells and down they came,
Struck again and then again.
Chimes rang out for all to hear;
Twelve O'clock arose a cheer.
Then behind closed doors they went
To rest until the next event.

Artist, draughtsman, patternmaker,
Moulder, founder, e'en tea-maker,
In the foundry men are toiling,
Casting iron that's nearly boiling.
Molten iron, straight from the furnace,
Streams down channels. Work in earnest!
In the Knockout, hammers clanging,
Shift the moulding-sand by banging.

The parts, assembled, made a clock
To grace the wall of solid rock,
Or was it brick, it matters not,
In Birmingham's old Bull-ring.
For many a year its chimes rang true
To cheer the shoppers going through
The Market Hall, if they but knew
Just what the world was brewing.

One dark night with sirens wailing,
Then on wing the threat came sailing
Over Birmingham in blackout,
Wardens shouting, 'Put that light out!'
Searchlights shining in the night sky,
Anti-aircraft guns had let fly
Missiles that would thwart the enemy
In the end, but not yet, anyway.

For tonight we'd take a pounding
Ere the all-clear sound was sounding.
Walls were broken, fire was raging,
Firemen, hoses fast engaging.
Soon the morning showed the trouble,
Pavements littered with the rubble,
Stock and fittings in the byways,
Glass and produce cloyed the highways.

Small boy stood in the ruined Hall
Oblivious to the costers' call,
Remains of what had been a stall,
Beneath his feet, now broken.
Gazed upon the shattered frame
Of the clock for which he came
But recently, to see the same,
Of life and times a token.

Older! Wiser! Disillusion,
Ushered in by war's intrusion.
Life is not a bed of roses
Floating in the reeds, like Moses.
Words of comfort, softly spoken,
Fail to mend hearts cruelly broken,
Whispered to grief-stricken mothers,
        Wives and sweethearts, sisters, brothers.

At his feet the clock, now silent,
Contrasts with the night so violent.
Casts a stone at one cracked bell.
Resonates a cracked 'Farewell'.

Jennifer

You sit down in your kitchen with a coffee in your hand,
Staring through the window, staring at the land,
The dishes waiting in the sink, the baby starts to cry,
But still you stare out blankly, a teardrop in your eye.

What happened to the little girl, with ribbons in her hair,
Who once believed in Santa Clause and fairies in the air?

One night a teenage party and the drinks began to flow
So just what happened to you, you really didn't know.
The candles burning dimly and the music playing loud,
What mattered for tomorrow so you joined in with the crowd.

You woke up in the morning; your childhood now was gone
And so had all the company who gladly led you on.
To face the world alone now, an aching in your heart,
For soon from home and loved ones you knew you had to part.

Your dreams of love and romance, they have faded with the
years.
Successive sugar-daddies merely graced your cheeks with tears.
No one to hold your hand now, no one to share your grief,
Just three small mouths preventing you from seeking quick
relief.

What happened to the little girl with ribbons in her hair
Who once believed in Santa Clause and fairies in the air?

One night a teenage party and the drinks began to flow
So just what happened to you, you really didn't know,
So you sit down in your kitchen now, a coffee in your hand,
Dreaming what life might have been the way you had it planned.

Happy and Pity

Oh, happy he
And happy she
On whom the reaper creeps
Without alarm,
He does no harm
But, taking one swift blow,
With perfect aim,
Frees the eternal spirit
From its weary frame.
For this he came.

But pity he
And pity she
Who, turning, sees the coming
Of the foe,
Parries the blow.
The battle lost, fights on.
Resists in vain,
Then bravely struggles hard
Not to complain,
Bearing the pain.

An Epitaph to Bounce

You were old, dear Bounce,
It had to be done.
You could not stand,
For your legs had gone.

The fields, we had roamed,
And the mountains climbed.
You ran on the beach
While the summer sun shined.

Twelve years we walked
And you played around.
You almost talked
With a growly sound.

I said it had to be,
And yet,
The day we took you to the vet,
Did I do all I could for you,
My four-legged friend,
To bring you through?

I feel a certain guilty qualm
To act like God; it brings alarm,
When I recall the love you gave,
That I should put you in your grave.
Remorseful tears well in my eye.
Goodbye, dear Bounce. Goodbye! Goodbye!

This poem was written by my mother, Dorothy Belcher, after the death of my father.

In Memory of My Husband.

If I could scan the deepest sea
Or wing to heights eternally
A message I would bring to thee
     Of my undying love.

The mountain peak with glorious scene,
The gaping gulf that lies between,
Could I but span the great ravine
     With my undying love.

Alas, this wish is not my gain
For longing only causes pain
To look for unknown realms in vain
     For my undying love.

How could I hope right from the start
For death prevailed and we must part
So now, locked up within my heart,
     Is my undying love.

Until that day when we shall meet
Together, at our Saviour's feet,
And find that joy that is complete,
     Our Lord's undying love.

Dolly's

They simply called it 'Dolly's'. As far as I remember it had no other name. It stood on the corner of two roads and was separated by a railway bridge from the entrance to the park. It was an unobtrusive building on the outside, the most prominent feature being two large shop windows displaying the word 'Refreshments'. Lace curtains covered the bottom half. The central door, set at an angle to the windows, emitted a loud 'clang' when opened and, inside, the counter formed a square which was in line with the door, that is, diagonal to the shop. There was usually a row of mineral-water crates lining the customer side of the counter. From time to time these came in very useful as seats.

Very few adults ever ventured inside, it was a kids' world. Second-hand comics could be bought for a penny and sold back for a halfpenny. Cardboard tubes with an elastic band over one end which made a funny noise when blown were threepence. One could buy ice cream, pop, or both together in a glass, toast, with or without jam on it, cakes, tea or coffee. It was, I suppose, the forerunner of the modern coffee shop, but there were no juke boxes, one-armed bandits or pin tables. It was rather the social atmosphere of the place that attracted so many youthful souls to crowd in and exchange their pocket money for a whole lot of fun. That, and the magnetic personality of Dolly herself.

The customers varied from pupils from the local boys' and girls' grammar schools to weary young footballers returning from play in the park. There was Millie, portrayed by one talented budding cartoonist as the 'Belle of Dolly's'. She was an attractive girl with naturally frizzy hair and the ability to defend herself from unwanted male attention by catching hold of the little finger and twisting it in a vice-like grip until a submission was obtained. There was 'Happy Horace', whose temperament was so changeable that he came in one day and bought a bottle of aspirins, the contents of which he swallowed completely and asked for more. Needless to say his request was refused. There was a lazy, fat boy who used to lie full length on the counter eating continuously. His one virtue was that he was very studious and thereby did well at school.

Vimtos were a very popular line; sometimes we drank them but, more often than not, simply shook them up and squirted them at one another.

Dolly seemed to be open at all sorts of hours and one day during summer a neighbour complained to the authorities. Now there was a purpose in this. Double Summer Time was in operation in those days so it did not get dark until nearly eleven p.m. The park closed at dusk and that was when we most urgently required Dolly's services. After the complaint she began to close the shop earlier, but still served jugs of tea over the wall at the back. The neighbour again complained that sales were being made after permitted hours, so we got our heads together. One evening an inspector arrived to catch Dolly passing a jug over the wall. What was in it? Water! Any law about giving away a jug of water? How the timing worked out so perfectly I never found out.

One day a sign went up 'For Sale'. Dolly was moving on. She had bought a chicken farm somewhere on the Shropshire border with Wales. In a short time the pop crates had gone and instead the shop was filled with neat, square tables having four chairs at each table. Only one trouble though, they were empty chairs.

The Why's Owl

In a tree in the shade lives a very strange bird
With a question-mark for a head.
He's never been born, and he's never been laid.
Or so it has been said.
His eternal quest, or perhaps you've guessed,
Is to ask the question 'Why?'
While the other birds sing, his questions ring
Throughout the ethereal sky.

"Why are we born and why do we live?
Why get old and die?
Why do men fight for a bit of land
With a river running by?
Why do homes break, while the feeble quake,
And tyrants rule instead?
Why are some born to a life forlorn,
Some lame, other sick in the head?

"Why am I such a Whys old bird?
Why do I always ask?
Why not forget, have no regret,
And just get on with my task?
But I can't, you see, 'cause it wouldn't be me
If I didn't have a try
At getting at the answers
By asking 'Why? Why? Why?"

In a manner like this, the bird's questions flow,
Seeking answers to all the world's woes.
While the other birds sing, his questions ring
For the answers that p'rhaps no one knows.

Raddimarraddle

There was once a man, back in 'fifty-four
And he couldn't eat
Any kind of meat
All because he'd got a broken jaw
And his wrist was fixed in plaster.

So I spoke to the man with the broken jaw
But he told me lies,
Which was not wise,
As he hissed through his teeth 'cause his gums were sore,
He related his disaster.

He said he was preaching the Christian word
When caught by the hair
And thrown down the stair.
It later transpired this was absurd
But he claimed to be persecuted.

The truth came out when he went to court
And faced the law
With a broken jaw.
His protestations came to nought
For the facts were undisputed.

He'd assaulted a boy, the charge was laid
But the father came out
With an angry shout.
He might have escaped; an attempt he made
As he jumped onto his saddle

But Pa grabbed a broom as the bike came by.
Straight through the front wheel!
The tyre gave a squeal!
The man with the jaw was in the sky;
Next thing he was raddimarraddle.

Biffer City

You'll excuse me for writing this ditty
Of a place that they call Biffer City,
Where they're so full of greed
They have more than they need.
They drive smart limousines
And they make big machines
To save work, so they think,
But to make them, they stink,
'Cause they toil, sweat and slave without pity.

The Biffers think always of money.
To me it seems really quite funny.
They make it, they take it.
They rattle and shake it,
Invest it, contest it,
But never detest it.
They lend it, they spend it
And often contend it
Is sweeter to them than pure honey.

It may be with me you will differ
But to get anywhere as a Biffer
You must think of your purse
From the pram to the hearse.
You must gather your pile
To enhance your lifestyle.
You must count every coin
And let no one purloin
That great heap just in front of your sniffer.

If Biffers don't count every penny
Then they're out on the street without any.
They will sleep in a door,
On a mat on the floor,
On a bench by a train,
Or just out in the rain,
In the cold and in pain
Till they're almost insane!
And I don't mean just one – there are many!

My Rough Book

A long time ago, when I was at school, I had a rough book, the purpose of which was to jot down notes, ideas, calculations, facts, etc. that were not ready for inclusion in my work books. At times, however, when lessons became intolerably boring, my rough book became a welcome outlet for the expression of pent-up mental activity, in visual form. Doodles appeared on its pages, sometimes in the form of patterns but, more interestingly, in the shape of strange animals, sometimes formed from novel uses of words and expressions.

Thus a menagerie of creatures evolved. There were, for example, Time-flies, depicted rather like house-flies with clocks on their backs. Maybees, Beelines, Crowflies, Bokowonko Birds (Don't ask me where that name came from) and, my favourite, The Why's Owl (There's only ever been one.) all appeared. Not surprisingly, inhabitants of this fantasy world later re-appeared as protagonists in some of my poems, as you will see.

The Time-Fly and the Wheelybug

The time-fly and the wheelybug
Went out one day for dinner.
Said W.B. "It seems to me
That you are getting thinner."

To this, the time-fly answered that,
As days were getting shorter,
He could not eat the kind of meat
That people said he oughta.

The meal consumed, with time to spare,
To talk, their one desire,
To rest their feet they took a seat
And sat down by the fire.

The conversation covered all
The things that are quite vital,
Like family trees and bandy knees
And why the weather's frightful.

The time-fly's job was making time
And he could make a minute
With such great skill he would not spill
A single second in it.

His grandfather, Old Father Time,
Had taught him with great courage,
With Breakfast Time and Dinner Time
(Kill Time was doing porridge).

The wheelybug jumped on his bike,
The time-fly spread his wings,
So now, well fed, they went to bed
To dream of pleasant things.

Two Crow-flies

Two crow-flies sat upon a wall
Engaged in making beelines.
They worked with speed, aware the need
To dodge marauding felines.

"The nearest way to get to Spain,"
The one said to the other,
"Is catch a plane or take a train."
The other wouldn't bother.

She'd rather go to Chesterfield
To see the twisted steeple
Or spend an hour at Blackpool tower
And meet some different people.

If it was nice, she'd travel east
To view the great monsoon
Or take a trip upon a ship
That goes straight to the moon.

Just then the beeline in her hand
Was caught up by a kitten
So off they flew, right out of view
Before they both were bitten.

     All crow-flies make beelines,
     Some thin and some thicker,
     However, you travel
     You won't get there quicker.

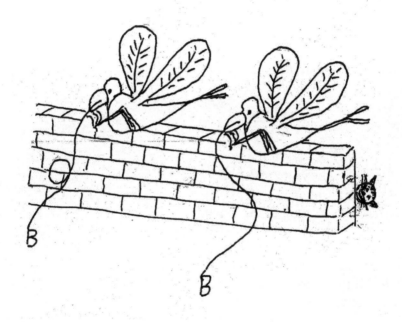

The Flight of the Bokowonko Bird

Way back before the world was born
There was no night and there was no dawn,
There lived a bokowonko bird
Who'd travelled far, or so we've heard.
These birds had purple, cat-like tails
And lived near enigmatic snails.

On his tail there was a tin-can, tied with care with plaited nylon.
In his beak he held a trumpet, shaped like an electric pylon.
With his claws he held a hammer and a tin of round-wire nails.
He had come to mend the cooker for the enigmatic snails.

The clanking tournament was on;
The polished cans all brightly shone.
Our hero strode into the ring
And silenced those who tried to sing.
The reigning champion there he faced
But knew there was no need for haste.

He could clank his can the loudest with a stick of seasoned
willow
Which he'd purchased with the money placed with care beneath
his pillow
By a kind and lovely fairy in exchange for one old molar,
There being no anaesthetic. For the pain, this one consoler.

A mighty swing he gave the willow,
The can, tough as an armadillo.
The noise rang out for all to hear.
Hurray! Rose the resounding cheer.
Alas, before he got the prize.
He had a terrible surprise.

Now he found there was one problem for the can was fixed with nylon
To his tail. In turn, his body sped behind. He dropped the pylon.
On he sped to outer regions, dropping nails. To end this ballad,
No one now to fix the cooker, that's why snails prefer cold salad.

Post Haste

The Time-fly used a motorbike
To take his love a letter.
He could have gone by Beeline
But the motorbike was better.

He skimmed around the corners
With the Maybee on his pillion;
When he reached forty miles an hour
It might have been a million.

Post haste he took the letter to
The one he'd set his heart on
And shared a creamy yoghurt
With her, from a plastic carton.

"Time flies" he said, "Must hurry home
Before the day is ended."
And so, with haste he rode away
Much earlier than intended.

A Fairytale that's True

Once upon a time there was a young tailor from London named Harold. His father had died and his mother found it a struggle to bring up her family of five children. When he was twenty years old a terrible war started, worse than any war the world had ever known.

Like many other young men, Harold joined the army to help bring the war to an end. Because he was a tailor and could sew he was sent to France and told to sew patches on aeroplanes that had been damaged in battle. Of course planes in those days were different from those we see today. They had a wooden frame, over which textile material was stretched and then painted. It was this material that Harold had to repair.

At his work he met a young leatherworker from Birmingham, named Bert. Before the war started Bert used to make leather seats for cars but now he also was repairing planes. Harold and Bert became good friends.

One day Bert, who was married, showed Harold a photograph of his wife's sister, Dorothy. She was pretty with dark hair. Harold wrote a letter to Dorothy and she answered it. After that they both wrote many letters to each other but, of course, they could not meet because of the war.

At long last the war ended and Harold and Bert went home. Soon Harold went to Birmingham to see Bert and to meet Dorothy. They fell in love and were soon married. After a time they had two children, first Nola, and then her brother, John. John, is the author of this book.

The Bokowonko Tournament

The Bokowonko Tournament
Is what I went to see
Sometime before the world was born
And the sun was still in the sea,
For ev'ry bird had a can on his tail
So bright and highly polished,
That was, of course, before
The Berlin Wall had been demolished.

The object of the tournament –
To make a lot of noise –
By hitting your can with a wooden stick,
It sorted men from boys.
The old guys used to talk about
The way it had been done
When they were young, so long ago,
Before the moon was spun.

"You young 'uns, in this day and age,
Don't know that you've been laid,
With nylon string to tie your can
And sticks all ready-made.
We 'ad to use our own bare beaks
To prise the contents out.
We didn't 'ave no tin-op'ners
Before the stars came out."

I wandered round the side-shows
Eating chips and candy-floss.
I bought a squeely teddy-bear
From an ancient albatross.
A bell went 'ding', a gun went pop',
The tourn'ment had begun.
The birds lined up with sticks and cans
Which really was great fun.

The preparations had been made
In garage, yard and shed.
Competitors had tuned their cans
With little time for bed.
Of course, you must allow the fact
That tin was not invented
So cans were made of something else
That wasn't eas'ly dented.

The first contestant lost his can,
The second lost his head,
A third one broke his clanking stick
And sulked off home to bed.
When rain stopped play at half-past-one
The site became deserted;
They rubbed their wounds with linseed oil
And bandaged where it hurted.

It's truly said, 'to run away'
Is good for the digestion
And, 'live to play another day'
A sensible suggestion
So, one day, when the tide is out
And sand goes on for ever
There'll be another tournament
No matter what the wevver.

The Wheelybug

There's nothing so cool when I've finished at school
   As I wheely along on my bike.
With my handlebars high and my head in the sky
   I just have to show off my new trick.
I can wheely around on the town cricket ground
   Doing circles and figures of eight,
And when I get home from an afternoon's roam
   I can wheely straight through the front gate.
If only they'd let me, I wish you would bet me,
   I'd wheely upstairs to my bed,
But they say "Wheely? Really? He must be mad nearly
   'Cause wheelying's gone to his head. Ha! Ha!
   'Cause wheelying's gone to his head.

There's nothing so bright in the first morning light
   As I wheely along on my bike.
When I hear the dogs bark and the song of the lark
   I jump onto my bike in a tick.
On a disused railway I can pedal away
   Doing slalams and speedway broadsides,
And upon my back wheel I can spin like a reel
   And fly like amusement-park rides.
One day, when I'm older, I'll be even bolder
   And jump over ten conker trees.
But they say "Conkers! Bonkers! The king of all plonkers!
   Go up and wash those dirty knees!"

Hill Walking

Hill walking has always been a passion of mine, the English Lake District being one of my favourite venues. The exhilaration of reaching the trig-point of a Lakeland fell bears no comparison with other forms of outdoor activity for me, not being a competitive type. There you are, tired and exhausted, sweating and breathing heavily, collapsing against a concrete or stone pillar, the original purpose of which was to make accurate maps, happily beholding, (visibility permitting *) a panoramic view of other peaks in the national park and considering which one you will attempt next.

On the way up you will, most probably, have met some interesting people and, perhaps, even gained a few tips about the remainder of your journey, You will have looked down on beautiful tarns, maybe a thousand feet below you, wishing you had wings like the birds that swoop overhead and possibly regretting that you do not have the courage to take up hang-gliding or para-gliding.

Not that majestic mountain peaks are the only way to enjoy hill walking, humbler hills like the Wrekin, Stiperstones, Long Mynd in my adoptive county of Shropshire, or the Lickey and Clent hills on the outskirts of my native Birmingham offer great opportunities to enjoy the thrill of this activity. In fact, there are hills not far away from home throughout most of the British Isles.

* A tip: Weather forecasting seems to have gained some degree of accuracy in recent years so, when looking at the forecast maps, look for indications of high pressure coming from the Atlantic, (Usually depicted behind the T.V. presenter's back). If you see a high pressure system coming this way, that's the time to take a chance.

Rambler's Rap

The rambling man is a free-born soul
With his map and his boots and his walking-pole.
He's out on a walk that will test his mettle
As he slashes off the top of a stinging nettle.

He stares at the top of a tree-covered hill
From a stile that was made down at Dudmaston Mill,
His senses alert to the birds' sweet choirs
As they vie for a place on the overhead wires.

The flies are a pest but he can't help that
So he flops them away with his old felt hat.
The scent of the pines is as incense rare
As the branches sway just above his hair.

A bridge 'cross a stream makes a resting place
So he scoops up some water just to cool his face.
Then one last effort and he's at the top
Of the hill that he saw when he made a stop.

The crowning glory of a day spent well
For the man with a goal and a tale to tell.
So back down a lane at a nice, steady pace
All set for the week at his working-place.

Trig-point Trevor

Trig-point Trevor, with his best endeavour,
Said he could climb any hill in any weather,
But his plans were thwarted
And he almost bought it
When he slipped on the Stiperstones
And froze in the heather.

Off to Kinder Scout,
"What's all the fuss about?
That hill's nothing to a guy like me."
But it caused a rumpus
When he lost his compass
And wandered round in circles
Until half past three.

Up in the English Lakes, "I've got what it takes.
There's no challenge that's too tough for me."
But the Old Man of Coniston
Could hardly keep his own hat on
When Trevor took a tumble
And skidded down the scree.

It happened on Ben Nevis that he fell into a crevice
So the helicopter rescue team was scrambled in a flash.
There they tried resuscitation,
But it led to shear frustration,
So they buried him in Birmingham
Beside a mountain ash.

Trig-point Trevor, now across the river,
Climbs The Delectables of Bunyan's pen
And at night, if you're all alone
And stay still by Trevor's stone,
You may hear the crunch of boots
Just now and again.

The Loner

Companions come, companions go,
They fade away like lambing snow,
Where they are heading I don't know
And I walk on, a loner.

A map and compass are my mates,
They guide me through some kissing gates
But 'ere a kiss my passion sates
My lot, I ween, a loner.

No one to question which-a-way
To go. No one to have a say;
No one to plan the coming day
So I go on, a loner.

Some twenty folks, a rambling date,
A backmarker to close the gate,
Soon to the pub, must not be late.
That's not for me, a loner.

An engineer from Tunbridge Wells
Companions me along the fells
But when the path divides he yells
'Goodbye, my friend', - a loner!

Upon the steps of bold Mam Tor
A schoolteacher from Withenshaw
A sweet flirtation, - could be more?
But I remain a loner.

There comes a fork; she takes the left.
My path is right so I'm bereft.
With solitude again I'm left.
I'm born to be a loner.

They ne'er complain of aching feet
Nor grumble when the rain turns sleet.
A brief relationship is sweet
As long as I'm a loner.

Companions come, companions go,
They fade away like lambing snow,
Where they are heading I don't know.
Still I walk on, a loner.

A Wartime Holiday

The Second World War was almost at a close. Allied forces, penetrating deeply into the heart of enemy territory, had succeeded in routing and totally disorganising what remained of Hitler's fighting force. It was only a matter of time before the demoralised, misguided individuals who had dedicated their energies to the establishment of the Third Reich were mercifully ordered to surrender, thus saving quite unnecessary additional casualties in the eleventh hour of the war.

On the home front an impoverished Britain was endeavouring to begin the long process of recovery from the malady of war. Some restrictions were being slightly relaxed. Coupons for clothes, food, sweets and other things were given increased purchasing power. Ice cream, or at least a poor substitute for it, began to appear on the market for the first time in almost six years and at last we were able to depart from our homes without lugging that infernal gas mask around with us everywhere we went.

My mother always associated holidays with the sea-side. This is how it had been before the war. If she had not seen, heard and smelt the sea she had not had a holiday. It is not surprising, therefore, that with Britain's coast forming one continual line of defence from Land's End to Land's End, we had not had a holiday since 1939. The general relaxing of restrictions made provision for the opening up of a small number of popular holiday resorts, particularly in the north, so, with this opportunity before us, the family decided to take a holiday in Blackpool.

It was with a lot of excitement that the day of our departure arrived. A number 18A bus took us to Alcester Lanes' End and either a 39 or 42 tram (What does it matter now?) took us to "Town", that was the expression everyone used for the centre of Birmingham some six miles away. Somewhere in Town was New Street Station and it was here that we joined an extremely large crowd of people all apparently bent on getting to

Blackpool. Everywhere pre-war buckets and spades were strapped to pre-war suitcases, and pre-war Kodak Brownie box cameras in faded brown rexine cases had been carefully dusted ready for use. At intervals unintelligibly garbled announcements from trumpet-shaped loud speakers were followed either by the screeching of brakes, as successive trains pulled up at nearby platforms, or by the heavy puffing of departing trains, valve gears in full forward position. Eventually a steaming, hissing black monster slid into our platform, forcing people at the front of the crowd to step back into the people in the middle of the crowd who, in turn, stepped back into us.

There were no vacant seats on the train so we ended up sitting on our cases in the guards van. For me, however, most of the journey was spent standing by the open window of the door; my holiday had already started.

On arrival at Blackpool we made our way to the boarding house where lodgings had been pre-arranged. It was a terraced villa, of early twentieth century design, standing in a short, straight road, itself part of a grid-pattern development typical of the period. The road came to an abrupt end, fenced off from the railway beyond by a row of old railway sleepers standing vertically. At intervals the fence was supported by sleepers, set deeply in the ground, protruding half way up the fence. These supports made an ideal platform on which to stand to watch the trains.

The reader will have gathered by now that the most outstanding impression this holiday left upon me was its association with the railway but there were other things. It was in Blackpool that I first noticed that white lines on the road were now being painted with some kind of thick cement paint that stood up in relief from the surface. I noticed that the sea was brown instead of blue as I remembered it from a pre-war holiday in the south. Tramcars were capable of running smoothly on rails without lurching from side to side as was usual on Birmingham's archaic system. I noticed the extravagance of the American soldiers thronging the streets; the gutters were littered with cigarette ends three-quarters of their original length. Austere years here had bred a generation of smokers who would burn their fingers before parting with a nub-end. There was the fair, enormous for those days, and the ghost train which was quite scary.

Of the rest of the holiday I remember little. There was a visit to the tower ballroom; we could not go up the tower. We went to Fleetwood, at that time a small fishing village. The time we spent on the beach and in the sea has been obscured in my memory by many similar experiences in subsequent years.

I have never returned to Blackpool for a summer holiday. Now that there is freedom to travel to places with more natural beauty, I have little desire. I once spent Christmas there and had my car stolen from the car park which now occupies the former railway marshalling yard where I had happily watched the trains so many years before, but still in my memory is stored a clear picture of a delightful experience during those closing days of the war.

Steam Locomotives
(A Rondeau)

In the fire they were created.
Men with sweat were saturated.
In machines the parts were groomed,
Assembled as an era loomed.
Soon the world they dominated.

Given breath by fire unsated,
Working folks emancipated,
Coal to smoke and ash consumed,
In the fire.

Executioner's torch awaited,
Now they lie with breath abated.
To the melting-pot now doomed,
Writhing, shapeless mass resumed,
To frames for buildings relegated,
In the fire.

Jools, the Genetic Engineer

There was a man whose name was Jools –
Worked in a lab with lots of tools.
He engineered things we call genes
And thus produced some bizarre scenes.

On oxtail soup he had a craze;
He ate it mornings, nights and days.
He took it with him on the train
And said it helped him use his brain.

One day his butcher gave him news,
That could have given him the blues,
Oxtails were now in short supply,
So Jools decided that he'd try
To make an ox that grew new tails,
And so, with hammer, screws and nails,
He set to work with great delight
And finished by the morning light.

He put his ox out in a field
And waited for the beast to yield
A tail that, when it was detached,
Would be replaced – a new one hatched.

He waited for a week or more
But still no tail at all he saw,
And then a funny thing took place –
The ox had got a spider's face!

The spider thought Jools was a fly
And chased him round the field, Oh My!
That night, before Jools went to bed,
He shot the monster, shot it dead.

But, morning-time, when Jools went round
To put the body in the ground
The animal had disappeared
And was at large, so Jools feared.

So, next time you go Joolses' way
Watch Out!

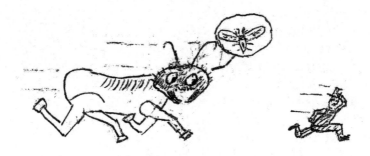

The Girl on the Beach

For a fleeting moment she was there, then she was gone.
I know I shall never see her again.
At the end of a hot day,
A tiring day,
She appeared, as from nowhere.
Her auburn hair,
Her blue denim skirt,
Her smile.
What were her thoughts as our eyes met?
Was it shyness that prevented conversation?
Was it modesty?
Would she, like me, like to have talked on and on into the night?
Or perhaps she was unconcerned, not even noticing I was there
So that I was never recorded on her memory.
She has close relatives,
A circle of friends,
A way of life.
Now she has returned to them,
But for a moment,
A fleeting moment,
She was the girl on the beach,
Full of untold secrets,
Of promise,
Of possibilities,
Of happiness or maybe of sadness,
Of new things,
Of future things,
Of dreams,
Of bubbles that burst when they are touched,
Of unreality.
Yet it is that kid of unreality that gives hope.
It can change to reality.
She might have become mine.
But no, not this time.

She walked off into the gathering dusk
At the end of a hot day,
A tiring day.
The beach is empty now.

Inspiration

An essay which I hope will help aspiring poets

There are, no doubt, those who can sit down with a blank sheet of paper, a blank mind and a couple of hours to spare and turn out a beautiful poem that will capture the imagination of readers and competition judges alike. I have to admit that, apart from a couple of cases, I am not one of them.

After the aforementioned period, my paper would probably be eligible for the Doodle of the Year contest, there would be few blank spaces left on it, but no poem. Perhaps, if I sat down with the intention of drawing doodles, a poem would appear, a novel idea, I will try it someday.

But, to be serious, I cannot work without what may loosely be described as 'inspiration'. Loosely, because it is a word which can be applied at different levels, from the giving of the Ten Commandments to the 'Eureka' associated with Archimedes' inspirational answer to his problem. Psychologists sometimes call it the 'Aha!' experience, meaning that all the bits and pieces were present in the mind all the time, waiting to be assembled into a 'whole'. If the well-known story is to be believed, Archimedes was not even working on his problem when he got the answer, he was having a bath.

This brings us to the most important factor concerning inspiration. It works quite independently of any conscious effort you may make to create an idea. All the material for your poem, whether learnt a long time ago or yesterday, is already in your mind then, suddenly, you see it standing out from the background and ready to be written down. Only then do you need to consult a dictionary or thesaurus to tidy up the details.

However, it would be wrong to give the impression that all you can do is to sit back and hope for something to happen. Nothing can come out of your mind that has not previously gone in, so it is important to develop an enquiring mind that takes an interest in a variety of subjects. Detailed observation of sights, sounds, smells and feelings will feed in lots of information which may come in useful someday.

Sometimes the darkest emotional experiences such as broken relationships, divorce, disenchantment, unfair treatment, pain, sorrow, bereavement and poverty can be turned into creative ideas that come from the heart. On the other hand, exhilarating experiences such as travel, beautiful friendships and the endless wonders of nature can provide just that input that will one day emerge as a poem.

The older we get, the greater will be our experience of life, so think about the many things that have happened to you over the years, maybe things that you laugh at now but did not find funny at the time, or people you knew in the past. Spend time dwelling on these things, then sleep on it. Hopefully, inspiration will do the rest.

So, if I cannot sit down purposefully and write a poem, when do I do it? Usually at the most inconvenient time. One poem was scratched on the back of a tea packet with a sharp stone as I stood in nostalgic contemplation by a lake in Cumbria. Another was pencilled on an old envelope as I sat on a stile. Yet another appeared on the back of an Ordnance Survey map as I observed the destruction of a sand castle on a beach. Sometimes I have to pull onto a layby and write. Nowadays I try to have writing material with me all the time, just in case, but sometimes I have to try to remember the gist until it is convenient to write it down.

Observation, then, is the key. It provides the input of material which, digested by the conscious and, perhaps more importantly, the sub-conscious mind, can be triggered into an idea which almost seems as if it was put there by an outside agent. This is inspiration. The words seem to appear mysteriously and all you have to do is to write them down. Often though, after a short while, you dry up and lose touch. This is the time to put it away and 'forget' about it. Strangely, the sub-conscious mind will often remember and may eventually turn up just the words you need.

If

If flames were black and smoke was red,
'A funny world!' the wise man said,
'I think we all should go to bed.
It's daft to talk like this.'
If peace on earth, for what it's worth,
Meant no more wars or unwanted birth
Of infants brought onto the earth,
Their lives so hit and miss.

Palestinian girl of sweet sixteen
Can blow herself from this earthly scene
Because she believes in something green
And pleasant after death,
But, for all that's known, she's gone to hell
(For who has been and who can tell
What motivates the darkest knell?)
For causing such distress.

The F. A. don't appoint a ref,
Who's nearly blind and partly deaf,
To judge a game that's played to death
By those who want to fight,
Whose sympathies are ever tied,
By fiscal links he tries to hide,
To boost the fortunes of the side
He thinks is in the right.

If we could eat and, in the street,
The rain was falling, and the sleet,
The puddles forming round our feet,
We'd all wish we were fish.
So, 'If', I say, and if one day
That 'If' should come along my way,
I'll write a poem that will say
The words I fondly wish.

Hey! Mr farmer

(A Triolet)

Hey! Mr farmer, what 'ya do wrong
When all that you did was protect your own?
They locked you up for Oh! so long.
Hey! Mr farmer, what 'ya do wrong?
For what you possess didn't come for a song;
You worked in the weather that would chill the bone.
Hey! Mr farmer, what 'ya do wrong
When all that you did was protect your own?

(N.B.)   This is one of two poems about this incident when a
         man, tired of constant robberies, shot the intruders and
         received a four-year prison sentence.

Social Suicide

Oh, Mr Martin what a shame
You only dropped the one who came.
If you had put them both down deep
You might have had a good night's sleep,
And other folks could rest assured
Another social evil cured.

Alas, the law does not judge right
The old instinct of man to fight
For what is his by work's reward;
He must not dare take up the sword.
He must stand by and see it stolen
And by such law the thief embolden
To carry out more daring crimes.
It is the lesson of our times.

The car thief who will run you down
With your own car is just dressed down.
A mugger preyed on your dear Nan;
He knocked her down and then just ran.
The arsonist burns down the schools;
Because he's nine we all look fools.

When will our politicians quake
And from this lethargy awake,
To get it firmly in the head
That social orders, long since dead,
When not put down by powers outside,
Committed social suicide.

Where are they All?

I walked around a cemet'ry
Where ev'ryone was good.
Up and down the aisles I wandered
Reading what I could.

"A loving husband, father, son"
A perfect guy, no doubt.
I sought in vain for stones that said
"Here lies a stroppy lout",

I thought I'd made a breakthrough
For one looked like "Badly pissed".
On close examination, though,
The words were "Sadly missed".

Where lie the drunkard wife-beaters.
Who plague this town, when fated
To occupy a plot in here?
Ah! P'raps they're all cremated!

The thought gave hope at last that I
Might sate my new obsession
So off I went up to the crem'
To do a history lesson.

I studied all the plates and plagues
With rapturous fascination,
But still not one gave me a clue
To end my odd fixation.

Where are the criminals and rogues?
Engravers must inscribe them
But nowhere could I find a line
To aptly thus describe them.

At last I gave up, packed it in,
No further point in trying,
But then it dawned on me that these
Inscriptions must be lying!

P.S   Since writing the above I have come across a memorial
         seat on the coastal path in Cornwall. I read the
         inscription, as I always do, and sat down. The plaque
         was in memory of a man who I prefer not to name, but
         whose nickname was 'Popeye',who lived from 1920 to
         1998 and whose epitaph reads:- 'Misbehaved all his
         life'. So there you are – ten out of ten for honesty!

Travel

After an untidy divorce, followed by unsuccessful attempts to build a new life, I left these shores to teach English in the developing world. For me, the 1980s was a period that broadened my experience of life on this planet but nearly killed me more than once. In Sudan when, near the 10,000 foot summit of Jebel Marra in Darfur, alone, starved and exhausted, I abandoned all my gear so as to reserve enough energy to fight my way across gorges of unstable volcanic ash to reach Gollol (pronounced Golool), where I could eat for virtually the first time in ten days. One slip on those near vertical walls, and this account would never have been written.

This period was the climax of my life, the emancipation of a wandering spirit that, perhaps had lurked inside me all my life. From the age of twelve I had wandered off on long cycling tours, sometimes accompanied, sometimes alone. By fifteen I had cycled, from Birmingham, south to Lands End and north to Carlisle, west to the Welsh coast and east to the North Sea.

It seems strange now but attitudes were different in the austere days just after the war. The present, perhaps justified, paranoia about the safety of children had not kicked in. We had freedom. I pity children of today, tapping away on tiny keyboards, communicating with people they can't see in the flesh or perhaps don't exist. Are they any safer than we were?

There were accidents of course, there always are. We used to take a ride on trucks pulled along rails by a cable connected to a stationary steam engine. The trucks were filled with coal and transported from the mine to the railway. The track crossed a main road by means of a tunnel. It was fun to ride on the top of the coal. One day a truck was loaded higher than usual and the boy on top was crushed against the low roof. He survived, but his spine was so damaged that he spent the rest of his life in a wheelchair. This kind of accident would not happen today; no-one is allowed near dangerous objects.

We used to go train-spotting at Tamworth, the nearest point the L.M.S. main line came to Birmingham. Nobody stopped us from putting copper coins on the line to see them elongated as the expresses thundered past, and nobody stopped us from putting our heads on the line to listen for the sounds of distant trains approaching. As far as I know, nobody failed to remove that member to a safe distance in good time. Are they any safer today?

There followed a period of relative stability when I became involved in fundamental Christianity which dominated my life for the next twenty years then, like the Why's Owl (see poem), questions arose and everything changed.

A Window Seat

I always like a window seat
When flying in a plane.
Let others watch the telly
While I search the coast of Spain,
Or watch the flares of oil rigs
In the night.

The desert dunes stand in relief
At sunrise and in gloaming
And ships at sea leave wakes so clear
They keep my heart a-roaming.
Towns scintillate in darkness.
What delight!

I look at clouds from up above,
It seems that I could land
Upon the cumulus below
And wave my arms and stand.
The thought both awes me and gives
Me a fright.

The shadow of our wingéd craft
Sweeps briefly o'er the snows.
The sun illuminates the Alps;
Each mountain summit glows.
A new respect for climbers
Clinging tight.

The stars above are crystal clear
There's little in between
The window and the orbs themselves,
So wondrous and serene.
A window seat reveals them
Shining bright.

At airports, taste the thrill of speed
Before we leave the ground,
As objects race across the view
And then there is the sound
Of landing-gear, retracting
Out of site.

You read your book or watch your film
And thus enjoy your leisure.
I, in my trusty window seat,
Derive a lot of pleasure,
And pass the time so quickly
On my flight.

They live on top of a Train

They live on top of a train, they do.
On top of a train they live.
No cosy beds
To rest their heads
Their past has gone
As the train rolls on.
It left Khartoum
At half past noon.
A night's gone by,
If they don't die
They'll be in Kosti soon.

The souk is first on their object list.
At first they go to the souk.
They scour the plates
In the market place;
A piece of fish
Left on a dish,
A half-drunk Coke,
A boiled egg yolk,
Some lentil soup.
The train goes 'Poop'.
It's true; It's not a joke.

Back on the train with haste they go.
With haste back on the train.
No great career
For them draws near.
What will become
Of ev'ry one?
Just boys they are
Who travel far
Without a home
Except the dome –
Shaped top of a railway car.

The Journey to Gezira Abba

I hurried along in the burning sun
To catch the last pontoon*.
My fastest was a walking pace
Through the sand of Kosti town.

I was on my way to visit James,
James, who all the while,
Lived a lonely life apart
On an island in the Nile.

His life was made more bearable,
We are to understand
By an honours degree in Arabic
He'd gained in old England.

'Twas many the time he'd helped me out
When I burst out like a bubble,
By speaking in the native tongue
He got me out of trouble.

A man was washing a horse one side,
His piece of soap was sinking.
The other side, a donkey boy
Collected water for drinking.

The water hyacinths blocked the ducts;
The engine lost its power,
But still we reached the Abba Isle
In just less than an hour.

A dusty road led to the town
Where lived my valued friend.
His home of mud-brick walls had brought
My journey to an end.

* ferry

The Journey to Ed Dueim

<u>Sudan 1980</u>

It was already dark by the time we had dug the 'bus' out of the soft, dry sand, shovelling and shoving until the groping tyres climbed uneasily out of the trenches they had created two hours previously. The darkness of the horizon, with neither moon nor stars to illuminate the night, was punctuated with vivid flashes of lightning, although we could hear no thunder.

We pressed on southwards into the rain, into the gathering storms. The lightning became brighter, the rain became heavier and the soft sand was soon immersed in streams of water, feet deep. We stuck fast in one of these wadis, sinking hopelessly up to the axles. One or two lorries passed somewhere near but, preoccupied with keeping their own vehicles moving, their drivers ignored us. A landrover ploughed through, advantaged by its four-wheeled drive.

Our vehicle was ill-equipped for emergencies. The piece of broken spring which we had used to dig our way out of the dry sand proved totally inadequate for the wet. There was no shovel, rope or winch on board. Thus, the driver decided we should stay there for the night.

The interior of the bus was so crowded that the four of us decided to sleep on the roof, the rain by now having been reduced to a mild drizzle. I tried to sleep but without success. With my eyes closed I became aware of a chorus of nocturnal sounds; the braying of donkeys, the 'more-more-more' of frogs, the barking of dogs and the sounds of some, as yet, unidentified nocturnal birds.

A lorry stopped. Someone dug us out. We climbed down from the roof and moved on about two kilometres only to stop at an impassablewadi where we caught up with the other lorries and the land rover stuck in the middle. We emerged from the steel-slatted door to find a hut built of mud with a straw-roofed annex supported on rustic timber poles. Glasses of tea were being served at a table, by the light of an oil lamp. It turned out to be a kind of transport café, a regular stopping-place for travellers, but in the present situation there was no choice but to stop.

In the darkness we discerned that we were on the edge of a village. The 'café' proprietor invited us into his living quarters, the oil lamp was brought in and a pack of playing cards produced. They taught us a game, we taught them one, large cockroaches crawling around us as we squatted on the straw mat that separated us from the earth beneath. They won, we won, all good sportsmen; it mattered not who won.

Our glasses were constantly refilled with tea and a small shop in the village sold us Pepsi-cola. It dawned on me that this was the real thing, not a reproduction of native hospitality for the benefit of tourists. These people were living almost as they had lived for thousands of years and we were their guests. The passing lorries had only slightly altered their lives – the shop in the village sold brake fluid.

We were invited to sleep on the floor of our host's house but thinking of the cockroaches, we politely declined and chose to return to the bus, cramming between the bench seating of this basic transporter with slatted sides and a leaky roof. It had been constructed with the emphasis on utility rather than comfort. Did it have any springs? I never found out! So far, passengers had accomplished most of the journey southwards from Khartoum, suspended midway between the wooden seats and the roof with frequent encounters with both. Even so they sustained less injury than the baggage which had been pulverised by our bodies as we alternated between weightlessness and an undetermined number of G forces. No fairground proprietor has ever conceived a ride to compare with our journey.

We emerged at dawn to find ourselves and the village on a peninsular of land almost surrounded by water about two feet deep. Friendly village children crowded round, eager to get on every photograph, thus a picture of a lorry stuck in water became a head-and-shoulders portrait and a village scene became a smiling group.

It had stopped raining but the water was still high and it was 1.30 p.m. before the driver plunged the empty vehicle through the water while we waded across. As fatigue set in we found it increasingly difficult to cope with the extreme jolting of the vehicle. Although we desperately needed sleep we had to stay awake to brace ourselves against the impacts we encountered on returning to our seats. Thus the remaining hours of the journey assumed a nightmarish character. It was, therefore, with great relief that we eventually reached Ed Dueim, the provincial capital of the White Nile Province, which had been our destination for twenty-eight hours.

In a Grey Mini

I spring to full consciousness
In a grey mini,
Sitting in the passenger seat,
Off the road, surrounded by trees,

Why am I here?
What is that, in my hand?
A capo, a guitar capo!

Why is my face wet with tears
And my eyes feel as if I have been in a prize fight?

I remember now.

"Separation," you say,
You want a separation.

Why now – on my birthday?
The day that filled my parents with so much happiness.
The day I was a star each growing year.
The day I became a man.
The day I bought a capo.
Why, on that day, do you break the news?

No answer to that!

"Where are we?
We should be home by now."

"I can't take you home in this state!"

Time heals – eventually – except on birthdays.

Ullswater Lament

Open your throttles, Raven,
Open them wide and roar,
So speed your way to Pooley Bridge
But I'll be on board no more.

Two years ago, my love and I
You bore across Ullswater,
But now she's gone, we'll sail no more,
And so's my son and daughter.

A lonely man stands on the quay,
Glenridding lies behind,
A car-park and some sailing boats,
A river to remind.

Like Raven, so my love's sailed on,
Just ripples on the shore
Remind me that she once was here,
But I'll be on board no more, no more,
I'll be on board no more.

Jebel Marra

The acacia thorn had penetrated the thick skin on the bottom of her heel and come out at the side of her foot just below the ankle. Using sign language she limped to me with the problem. The nearest town was nearly a day's journey away, maybe there was a hospital there but it might as well have been on the moon as far as this teenage, country girl was concerned. Maybe there was a witch-doctor somewhere near but, whether his treatment would cure or kill, is a matter of conjecture. A dilemma – if I tried to get it out and it broke, septicaemia or gangrene may set in and could lead to death. Leaving it in would have the same result.

In our society, with its 'claims culture', no-one outside the medical profession would dare to intervene in a case like this, neither is there any need, but the rules are different out there. The thorn was about four inches long and fairly thick at the bottom end. Decision made, I got her into a position where it was possible to get a firm hold on the thick stub sticking out of the bottom of the heel, looked at the angle it had gone into the flesh, tried to get in line with it and, gripping with all my might, gave a massive wrench. It came out whole. Whew! I don't know who was most relieved, me or the girl.

It was my first holiday in the Sudan. Several months of burning, inescapable heat, day and night had created a desire to go somewhere cool. Three days and nights by train along a dodgy track, from time to time littered with upturned coaches and trucks that had failed to remain on the rails, took me to Nyala in the west. There, I boarded a lorry bound for Nyama, a German work camp on the border of Jebel Marra. Jebel is Arabic for a mountain or hill, there is no separate word. There are big jebels and little jebels but they are all jebels. The Company was engaged in building an expensive main road that didn't appear to go anywhere of importance. It was rumoured to be a political whim. There I slept, laying my sleeping bag on a concrete slab outside one of the buildings.

Up at dawn, another lorry took me to Tour, a small village at the side of the new road, where a bridge is being built to span one of the seasonal springs that abound in the area. Here, I started the five mile walk to Gollol.

The air was fresh and I felt great. The path made its way through fields of grain, a local cereal used to make aseeda, a heavy pudding which is the staple diet in these parts. Footsteps came behind me, a girl, careless and casual in manner, overtook me on the path. As she did so, she thrust a length of sugar cain into my hand and then disappeared into a field. In an hour or so more, I reached the government rest house at Gollol, a substantial building set between tall trees, the land behind it climbing steeply towards the mountains.

The next morning I set out along a good track for the waterfall which tends to be the ultimate goal for the more casual tourist. It was magnificent and, for me, the gateway to further wonders.

Unable to obtain a map of the area, I had previously met some German walkers who had provided a pen-drawing copied off another drawing which had originally been roughly sketched from a very rudimentary map which showed little detail, and trusting the remainder of my life and well-being to this totally inadequate piece of equipment, struck out toward a cornfield and a tall tree that could be seen about fifteen miles away from a high point.

The mountain before me looked deceptively like Snowdonia. It was easy to forget that its 10,000 foot summit was part of the rim of a volcanic crater, probably about fifteen kms in diameter and, geologically speaking, of recent formation.

I felt carefree, a great adventure lay ahead although, had I known at that time what to expect, my feelings may have been different. How blissful it is to be kept in ignorance of the future. I was ill-equipped for the journey, assuming that it would always be possible to buy food from villagers. I had not been able to plan a route because I did not know in advance where it was possible to get by lorry, but I had a general idea of crossing the whole area from south to north, terminating at Nyertiti and back onto the road.

Kallokitting appeared to be the first sizeable village on route although there was no path shown on my 'map'. I passed a few very small villages, buying some tomatoes and an onion. The lady providing them apparently thought I was paying too much so she went and fetched another handful. I passed through fields of peanut plantations, trying to buy some products but being given them instead. Such was the generosity of these people who would not take any money at all. I passed through a shady glade where several white, furry monkeys scampered for refuge when they saw me. I sat still and waited for a long time but they would not come near.

When the sun fell low in the sky it became clear that, although I was heading safely in the direction of Kallokitting, there was no chance of reaching it before nightfall. I came to a small village called Kullokulla, a hamlet of a few round stone houses with thatched roofs. Near each house was a shelter consisting of a straw roof supported by four poles. Two of these poles were adjacent to the grass wall enclosing the compound, so reasonable shelter could be obtained. I met a boy driving his donkey up to the village, having filled his leather bottle with water at a nearby stream. He was a student at secondary school, presumably a boarding school, and could speak quite good English. We soon became friends. His hospitality could not be faulted, I had all I asked for and, in addition, a guided tour of the surrounding countryside.

On the morrow, before departing, he took me along the stream to show me the gardens belonging to the villagers. Here we picked grapefruits, oranges and lemons, eating a number of them before loading a bag to take with us. We enjoyed the day so much that barely two hours of daylight remained to make the journey to Kallokitting, and so, taking a donkey which we each rode in turn, the boy guiding the way, we arrived at dusk. At the rest house we met some more Europeans travelling in the opposite direction. They had previously bought donkeys to carry their gear along the tough mountain tracks but now, not needing them both, I bought one hoping it would ease my journey onwards. The animal was young and tired so I found him some good green pasture and let him rest the following day while I went, on foot, to Tora and followed the stream to a beautiful waterfall cascading down a gorge of rich, pink granite into a deep pool beneath. I stripped and swam in the cool, clear water before making my way back to Kallokitting. I passed several monkeys in the trees; the same white furry kind I had seen earlier. I studied the ingenious irrigation canals built by the villagers to channel water from the stream to their gardens. Here water was plentiful but further downstream toward the village it became less and less until it disappeared completely from the surface, leaving a dry, gravel bed some thirty yards across in which the villagers dug holes for water.

Next day I saddled up to my donkey and set off early for Torratonga, a good days' walk away. My horsemanship, or donkeymanship if you like, has never been renowned. Any attempt at riding or even attempting to establish rapport with these four-footed animals has usually ended in disaster and this encounter was to be no exception. Four hours were wasted covering the first mile so I sold him to a local at a considerable loss and continued on foot.

After a mile or so the path entered an eerie gorge of volcanic ash, its lofty sides pocked with holes, some taking on the appearance of grotesque faces mocking the lone traveller as he stepped beneath them. I pressed on into the gorge passing many branches of less significance and keeping to what appeared to be the main path, a path which became increasingly narrow as time went on. Suddenly, it stopped, completely stopped. With high walls surrounded, the only way out was the way I had come. Retracing my steps, I tried another and another and another with the same result. Hard rock can be climbed but this volcanic ash was too loose for that. The faces above were really mocking now; how many travellers had they caught in this weird maze?

Four hours had been wasted with the donkey and about the same in the gorge. Africa has almost no twilight; someone switches the light off at about six o'clock and, if there is no moon, it's dark – very dark. Retracing my steps to the last small village I found some village men drinking a potent home-made brew. One of them gave me accommodation and asked me if I could give him a shirt in return for his favours. This was difficult as I was only carrying two and one was in use. He would not accept cash at first but after his friends had left, he did so. He then showed me to the path to Toratonga.

Reaching Toratonga just before nightfall I realised, for the first time, how much I needed a cooking pot. Up until then I had not needed one but now things were different. For one thing the villagers were not so friendly and accommodating. I found a hut which I thought was the rest house. It had a corrugated iron roof and branches on the floor. Some youths came and told me it was not the rest house, that was about a hundred yards away in the woods, a rat-infested building with a thatched roof and concrete floor. A family of cheeky kids looked through the windows and door and would not go away. Outside was a memorial stone, inscribed in English with the names of victims of an air crash on that spot in 1960. I moved back to the shack from whence I had come. It was more peaceful and proved to be watertight, too, as there was a torrential storm in the night.

One of the youths, who had directed me to the rest house proper, managed to borrow a leaky old pot and ungraciously fetched some rice and cooked it, eating most of it himself and charging an enormous fee for the errand. Eating with him was an ordeal as he had some acute infection of the nasal passages and no means of disposing of the mucous thus generated but I was hungry and must eat. Little did I know that this rice would be my last meal for a long time.

The path passed through a narrow canyon which the rain had carved in the thick layer of volcanic ash, in places only just wide enough for a man or beast to get through. I noticed that I was following some newly-made cat's footprints. They measured 8 cms long by 7 cms wide. I followed them for several hundred yards, knife in hand, and nervous of every hidden turn in the path but the maker of the prints did not appear. Several baboons swung in the trees above me, keeping their distance. At one point I walked face to face into a wolf who immediately turned and fled, more credit to his quick reactions than to my bravery.

Before entering the crater itself I met the goatherd who lives there. One family only in this immense area of land. He was driving his herd along the path and I realised why the wolf was in this vicinity. I continued to walk across the crater, feeling an infinitely small spec in this vast creation.

A sulphur lake formed an arc on one side of the crater suggesting that subsequent seismic activity had tilted the whole area to one side. In the centre of the large crater stood a conical mountain. Later, from a viewpoint high on the main crater rim, it was clear that this was the rim of a crater in its own right, containing a blue lake about a mile across. I stood transported in silent wonder at this view, grieved that I had used all the film in my camera. I was not to know that this awe-inspiring view, the zenith of my life, was nearly to become my last.

Below me to the north, was a gently sloping plateau of volcanic ash. Seasonal rains had dissected it into vertical sided ravines running from south to north. After my previous encounter with similar ravines I determined that, on no account would I venture there. As it became dusk, I happened upon a large rock pool bordered by a level area containing some dry tinder. A good place to camp so, lighting a fire and making a wood pile near my head, I crawled, rather hungry, into my sleeping-bag and alternately slept and made up the fire so as to deter uninvited guests.

Next morning I began to feel the weakness caused by several days exertion and insufficient food. There was still no sign of a path to Nyertitti and there appeared to be no villages where I could buy food. About a mile from my camp, with the mountain on my left becoming steeper and the gorges on my right getting nearer, I saw two boys near a thorny sheepfold. With difficulty I descended the rocky slope and joined them on the edge of the ash plateau. I asked for food. Could they provide aseeda for me? The elder boy said something to the younger and the latter disappeared over the edge of the field. A few minutes later he returned with a filthy dish half-filled with filthy milk, obviously watered down. I drank it and paid the exorbitant price he demanded. For a further fee he offered to guide me on the right path to Nyertitty. He carried my load for about half a mile along a winding path, leaving me at a point where he said the path went straight on to Nyertitti, he collected his money and disappeared. I continued to follow the path to where it branched several ways, each way petering out and leaving me facing due north deep down in the system of gorges that I had decided to avoid at all costs. It now seemed impossible for me to reach Nyertitti and stay alive so, reluctantly, I decided to circumnavigate Marra on the west side and make for the point where my epic journey had started but as these gorges ran from south to north, I could find no way of going in the right direction. I decided to press on in a northerly direction hoping that all these gorges ran into one 'master' gorge stretching from east to west. Finding a stream, I followed it for miles through a deep ravine so narrow that at times I had to squeeze between rocks. It eventually turned east so I had to think again.

My brain was now suffering from lack of nourishment. I was vaguely aware of a lack of good judgement and an almost complete lack of a sense of danger. At times I would find myself perched on a narrow goat track right on the edge of a canyon, the ash under my feet barely able to support my weight, and yet not feeling any fear that a fall, even if not fatal, would certainly immobilise me and leave me to a worse fate.

Sometimes I had to carve my way through deep undergrowth in the bottom of the gorges and, although I knew that creatures capable of inflicting death may be lurking there, I pressed on with little regard for safety. A snake bite could be fatal, I knew, but I had to press on before my strength ran out altogether.

My memory of that day and the next is fogged, details having either never been recorded or soon obliterated in the fight for survival. I know I climbed up and down, along and round, over and over again as I tried to make my way back to the mountain. Here I would try to follow the contours around Jebel Marra itself and make my way over the col between Sawa and Marra, down to the path leading to Gollol. It was a drastic decision, made by a very weakened brain, but it undoubtedly saved me. By evening I had successfully made it to the edge of most of the ash gorges and stood at the foot of the massive crags of Marra. After twelve hours of the most strenuous walking I have ever done I was at a position barely three or four miles from my camp of the previous night.

The crags ahead were totally impassable for me so I was still forced to negotiate ash gorges at the foot of them. I climbed one of them at sunset. The top of the ridge was barely six feet wide and beyond lay a dark abyss.

Completely spent, I crawled into my sleeping-bag, sealed the open end with my broad-brimmed straw hat, which provided ventilation while keeping out unwelcome intruders, and fell into a fitful sleep disturbed by bad dreams. I had no fire, food or shelter and was glad it did not rain. It was then that a thought transcending all others imposed itself on my mind, a danger which made all other perils seem insignificant. I saw the face of my estranged but still loved wife. I had carried a hope that somehow, somewhere, it might be possible to make a fresh start. Long did I weep and call her name to the mountains. The thought that I may never see her again fired me with new determination. I would get home somehow.

At the crack of dawn, abandoning all my gear except my wallet, compass, knife and camera, and leaving a letter in my rucksack, more likely to be consumed in seasonal fires than ever to be found, I began my desperate attempt to reach Gollol that day. Details of my fortunes and misfortunes are only vaguely recorded in my memory but I do know that I negotiated another small series of ash gorges before gaining higher, rockier ground. From there, on the flanks of Marra, to my delight I could see, in the distance well below me, the snake-like path leading from Sawa waterfall in the direction of Gollol, but many were the obstacles still to be encountered before reaching that place of relative safety.

For a start I was on the wrong side of the ravine carrying the stream leading to the waterfall. I made my way down into the canyon near its top end and had to decide whether to follow the stream down or climb up the other side. I was to find out that writers of books on walking are correct when they say it is not advisable to follow streams down from mountains. After a mile or two the stream bed ended abruptly at an incredible drop into an even deeper ravine below. Gingerly peering over the edge of this waterfall, dry at the time, I gazed down at the tops of great birds of prey winging their way around in the void below me.

Retracing my steps a short way I found a place where the walls were not quite so vertical and, thankful for having abandoned my gear, managed to climb to the top. As it happened it was the last main obstacle conquered. Other valleys had to be crossed or contoured but they were not too bad and, on average, it was downhill. The steep descent was covered in dense undergrowth which tripped me up several times. On one such gambol I lost my sheath-knife. Even at this stage I still feared that a snake bite or a broken limb might be fatal but suddenly I burst out of the eight foot high grass onto the footpath to Gollol. The track was like an old friend. Wearily beginning the four-mile plod I soon passed the tree where I had romantically carved two sets of initials several days before. Later, I arrived at the rest house where my epic walk had begun, a bedraggled character with two weeks growth of beard and a belt buckle that was exploring new holes in the leather.

Although ravenous, the sumptuous meal that the kindly warden put before me was far too much for my shrunken stomach to ingest. The next day, the warden and I rode on donkeys to the site of the projected new road where I was able to procure lifts back to Nyala followed by a three-day train journey back to Kosti.

The Gate

I hope in vain, with tempered ear,
The sound to dry the glistening tear
But somehow know I will not hear
The scraping of the gate.

Ill-fitting gate in time-warped frame,
Each time it opens, just the same,
Has been like that since first I came.
One day I'll fix that gate.

This place beside the flowing Nile
Has been my home for quite a while.
Maybe you'll come and see my style
Behind that wooden gate.

I hear your hand upon the latch.
I check my dress is up to scratch.
"At last," I think, "Our lives we'll patch,
Together through the gate."

I must pretend it's no surprise
To let you see, it is not wise,
The light that glows within my eyes.
"When will you mend that gate?"

You play me at my own sweet game,
Pretending that, in truth, you came
With no real motive that you name,
Remarking on the gate.

There really is a scraping noise.
Reality my dream destroys.
"Sabbah Al Khier," a voice says, "Kwoiz?*
Mohammed shuts the gate.

* Arabic: Good Morning! Are you well?

The Gate – Original Version

What vain hope is it
That prompts me to listen for the scraping of the gate,
The ill-fitting gate in the ill-fitting frame?
It takes more than a little effort to open it.
Could you open it?

I see you, hand on the latch, shoulder against the wood.
I hear you, "Whew" scrape! "Uh! When are you going to get that
repaired?"

Imagination.

I pretend it is an everyday occurrence,
Or, at least, that I am not surprised to see you.
"Hello! Did you have a good journey?"
"Thought I would never find you," playing me at my own game,
"Phew, isn't it hot?"
"About 110° in the shade. I'll show you the shower.
Be careful, the water burns.
The pipes run in the sun."

You shower!
I think!
I remember!
Could it last this time?
You've made the effort.
Taken the initiative.
Travelled nearly 4,000 miles.
Dealt with the bureaucracy.
Had all those jabs – That convinces me.
You really mean to make it last.

The declining years lie ahead,
We are not young anymore,
Do we really want to face them alone?
Not me – no one could fill the gap.
And you. Your friends have deserted you.

There it is! Scrape! Scrape!
I rise from my clammy bed,
Struggle clumsily with the mosquito net,
Sheath myself in a shirt.
Dark patches appear immediately.

"Oh, Good morning, Mohammed, I mean erSabbah Al Khier."
"Kwoiz?"
"Kwoiz!"

Reality.

Divorce plus Five Years

Even now,
Sometimes,
I think it is all a bad dream,
That, one fine morning,
I will wake up
To the song of the birds in the trees,
To the bright sunshine of life on my face
And to the warmth of your body
Next to mine,
Beside me.

I will hold you tightly,
Clutch you so that you will not go.
You will ask me why I am so passionate.
I will tell you my dream,
Clinging! Clinging!
You will not fully understand
But you will calm me,
Telling me that all is well,
It is only a dream.

South from Kosti

The vessels forming the convoy had been lashed together, one on each side and three in front of the engine boat. The passengers, human and animal, were already aboard. Bread was drying on the upper deck and meat was hanging from rails on the lower deck. Canoons (charcoal cookers), made from recycled cooking-oil tins, were already alight on the decks.

Fascinated by engines of all kinds, I stood between the two ancient six-cylinder diesels as the engineer hand-cranked the donkey engine that would compress air to start the British-made monsters.

The school term had ended and we were setting out on the two-week journey from Kosti to Juba, the farthest you could go south on the Nile on anything other than a canoe. We had a cabin of sorts, filthy and cramped, so we chose to lie on the deck beneath the stars, between the rows of drying bread, listening to the throbbing of the great diesels, the grinding of the steering chains, the bleating of sheep and the sounds made by chickens, goats and people.

The further south we travelled, the more verdant became the landscape. Naked children ran along the banks and sometimes people would throw gifts of corn cobs. One hit me on the side of the face with unbelievable force. At intervals, rows of wooden stakes were hammered into the river bed to form semi-circles against the river bank. These, I learned, were to protect the women from crocodiles when they were washing or getting water.

This was the land of the Dinkas. Tall and lean, they herded their off-white cattle, with dewlaps hanging from their necks, along the green floodplain of the Nile. The cattle were their wealth; they had little need of money. Horns of these animals were often seen erected on trees or poles near the villages.

One morning I woke up to a different landscape. We were surrounded by green papyri about fifteen feet high with heads about two feet in diameter. We were in the Sudd, the massive swamp that stymied the Victorian explorers who attempted to find the source of the Nile. From the upper deck we could see over the top of these giant plants. They stretched to the horizon in every direction, a sea of green.

At one point the flotilla came to a halt in the middle of nowhere. Then we saw the bizarre scene of a woman, sitting on a kind of throne, high above the water on a floating raft of papyrus. She seemed to be of some importance, a queen perhaps. She was giving orders and was obviously in charge of affairs. Dugout canoes appeared from a channel in the standing papyrus and, for an hour or so, trade was conducted between the woman and our craft. Goods were passing in both directions. It was difficult to get a clear view of the proceedings but I saw dried fish coming aboard. Other merchandise from the ship was loaded into the canoes which seemed to be providing a shuttle service to some village which was hidden from our sight.

Shortly after this I went down with malaria, a severe form that makes the urine go black and does its best to destroy the kidneys. One of my travelling companions, Jonathan, was the son of a Harley Street specialist who had prepared him well for such an emergency. My body was put into the cabin while my mind drifted off into Cloud Cuckoo Land and Jonathan plied me with medicines which, I am sure saved my life. Well done Jonathan! Needless to say, of the rest of the journey, I remember very little.

On arrival at Juba we got a taxi to take us to the hotel. It drove around for twenty minutes or so, we alighted, paid the driver, who quickly disappeared. We looked down the road and there was our boat about a hundred and fifty yards away. No wonder he was in a hurry to get out of sight!

Two of our group of four who had left Kosti together, had disembarked on the way and proceeded to walk an incredible journey across the desert to the south west. The other decided to stay a while in Juba so I, still some way from recovery, continued my journey southward alone.

The road frequently passed over narrow bridges with no walls at the side and only just wide enough for the lorry on which I was travelling. The driver was obviously very drunk and some women passengers were banging on the top of the cab in an effort to make him slow down. At the first opportunity we all got off and waited for some less life-threatening transport to come along.

It was Christmas, high up in the Imatong Mountains near the borders of Sudan, Uganda and Kenya. A government-sponsored experimental scheme to grow eucalyptus (gum) trees for use as fuel, dominated the small village where I was welcomed into the brick-built home of an employee of the enterprise. A battery-powered tape recorder provided the music for a party where we danced, in the dim light, to the sound of Boney M. I was then accommodated on the veranda, protected by a fine wire-mesh screen from mosquitoes but not from rats, who seemed to find their way in to spend the night nibbling on the corn cobs stored there. Chomp! Chomp! Chomp!

In the morning a sheep was killed. Where the body went, I don't know, but the head was cooked and grinned at us from the dinner table. I was a vegetarian that day.

An old man died in the village. His shrouded body was dumped off the back of a landrover by a European employee of the Company. We dug his grave, taking turns with the one available implement, a metal rod with a flattened end about two inches wide. Still recovering from malaria, at seven thousand feet above sea level, breaking into the rock-hard earth was an exhausting task. The other grave-diggers seemed to fare little better so the grave was shallow and small. Hence the body was placed in a foetal position, the grave filled in and then we all placed our hands on the tool, for water to be ritually poured over them to cleanse away any trace of evil spirits that may have taken this opportunity of slipping into our world. I was then taken to the mud hut of the bereaved family to offer my condolences, and we drank tea.

After congenially departing from my hosts, I moved on a few miles along the mountain to another village where everyone was occupied in what appeared to be a non-stop dance. My face was painted white, like everybody else, and I simply joined in.

A lady brought a sick baby for me to bless, quite an emotional challenge at the time because I had recently gone through an uncertain period in my own faith and was all mixed up. I did not want to be a hypocrite but neither did I want to disappoint the woman. I evaded the issue but, with hind-sight, I think I should have blessed the child, hypocrisy or no. After all, no harm could be done. I just hope he survived.

Having descended the mountain, I decided to visit Luka who I had met on the way up. He worked for another government scheme and was provided with a small brick house. It was approaching New Year now. There was hardly anything to eat in the village and nothing at all in Luka's house apart from a very large bottle of aragy, a potentially lethal spirit distilled from dates. We talked on into the night, tippling on our empty stomachs until I went to sleep with my head resting on my arms on the table. I woke up to find that Luka had gone to bed and I was paralysed from head to toe. With no option, I went back to sleep and woke up in the morning in the same position but mobile. That has been my only experience of being paralytic drunk.

We went into the village. There was a butcher's stall but all he had was some fly-infested lungs and windpipes hanging from a horizontal pole. I kept my hunger.

Back in Juba, I returned to Khartoum by air and then to Kosti by lorry. I was violently sick on the way. I was not to know until four years later that my right kidney had been severely damaged and, after another bout of malaria, in southern Africa, was found to be completely blocked with scar tissue. Surgery partially restored its function.

A Dry Wadi

I don't know what to write today.
My mind's like a dry wadi.
(That's Arabic for streams that sometimes
Flow in desert places.)
I'd like to find a wet one now
To cool my tired body.
Instead, I'm in a desert
Full of unfamiliar faces.

It takes me back two full decades
When I was in Sudan.
Divorce had raised its ugly head
And blame was fixed on me.
Why wait to prove my innocence?
I simply turned and ran,
And started teaching English
In a town that's called Kosti.

To end this saga, limited
To thirty lines on paper,
Would tax the ingenuity
Of Gungadin and better.
Suffice to say, the next two years
Turned out to be a shaper
Of quite original ideas
Sent home in every letter.

Happy is the man or women for whom love comes in harmony with the circumstances of his or her life but sorry is the lot of those for whom there can be no consummation. Does that guy called Cupid sometimes get it wrong?

We sat beneath the Stars

We sat beneath the stars,
      There was no moon,
And talked the midnight hour
      Away so soon.
Time stayed its hand awhile,
      For us a boon
         From life's ordeal.

A Velia my dreams
      To so enhance.
Could such a joy have happened
      Just by chance?
Are fantasies essential
      To romance?
         But she was real!

Must moments such as this
      Pass by so fleet,
As sand castles are trampled
      Under feet,
And never more our trysting
      To repeat?
         Time will reveal.

On Acton Field

Tiny snails, half hidden in the uncut grass,
A myriad pastel shades
Illuminate their slender, twisted shells.
How vulnerable are they!
As campers cut across to shower away
The dust and sweat of a hot summer's day
On Acton Field.

How cruel the fates; two hearts entwine.
Was Providence so drunk with wine,
Or was it just some foolish jest,
An evil fairy's ill behest,
To bring together in one place
The ancient and the fair of face
And bind their hearts in perfect love
That fadeth not though, like a dove,
Each soars away to realms unknown
With no address or telephone
From Acton Field?

My heart, like mollusc, guarded by a shield,
Tempered by the years it would not yield,
Now stripped of all its armour on this field,
On Acton Field.

On the Stiperstones

I sit high on the Stiperstones and stare
Where legend says the Devil has his chair.
The sparkling quartzite glistens all around
Awakened from its sleep beneath the ground.
Geology!

My thoughts are on that weekend in July.
Three moons have passed and still I wonder why
I let that moment pass, how sad I feel,
I did not take you then and seal the deal.
Your lips were waiting, ripened by the beams
That shone without abate through what now seems
Eternity!

We tried to say goodbye as ev'ning fell
And close a chapter in our lives as well
But, e'cr we parted, tears began to flow
As rain surplants the beauty of the snow.

A journey into Paradise I'd missed
To cherish in my mem'ry, had we kissed,
But I was slow and left your lips intact
And now, in fantasy, I re-enact
That moment, how it should have been, in fact,
A memory!

From Biblical times to the present day, history has given very little acclaim to heads of state who have not been involved in at least one war during their time in office. William would not have been The Conqueror, Alexander would not have been Great, Ivan would not have been Terrible and Napoleon's repute would have been even smaller than his stature had it not been for the wars in which they engaged.

Could this be the reason why the Gulf War was fought? We were clearly told a lot of lies about weapons of mass destruction and duped into supporting a war which has apparently benefitted no one, 'apparently' because there are undoubtedly some who continue to live very comfortably on the proceeds of the arms industry and other recondite activities associated with war. The following group of poems were written just before and during the Gulf War.

Hans Blix

Hans Blix was a man with a mission
To find, in whatever condition,
Some weapons so awful,
So ghastly, unlawful,
His was an important position.

He searched to the south,
He searched to the north,
He searched to the east,
To the west he went forth.
He looked under lorries
And buses and trains,
He dug in the sand
And he poked in the drains,
He searched and he sweated
And tortured his brains
But nothing whatsoever
Was found for his pains.

Then, suddenly, one day, permission
Was withdrawn by some smart politician.
"We're starting a war;
That's what its been for.
Never mind the result of your mission."

Who Knows?

Said Mr Bush to Mr Powell
"A threat is on its way.
If we don't act to stamp it out,
We'll rue this very day."

"I know," said Colin, all perturbed
"We must do something quick,
Or else our world supremacy
Will soon go down the nick."

And so the pair devised a scheme
To nip things in the bud.
Saddam Hussein just sitting there –
With weapons – that was good.

He took the bait, did Mr Blair,
He swallowed it completely,
Together with the line and float.
They hooked him in quite neatly.

So now, in two decades from hence,
Europe remains divided.
The U.S.A. still reigns supreme
Because the threat's subsided.

No One Wins a War

Let's see who's losing the war today,
I press 'One' for the news,
Relax in comfort in my home
But can't escape the blues.

I tried to warn them, yes I did,
In letter, song and verse,
Before the first poor sod
Was lifted, lifeless, to the hearse.

For I'm an old one, I was bombed
Because the world went wild,
Surveyed in school the empty seat
Where yesterday sat a child.

I've lived and worked in the Arab world;
I know what makes them tick.
To think they'd just accept defeat
Is naïve to the point of sick.

"It will take longer", we are told,
"Than we at first believed."
Then, someone got their sums all wrong
Or, more likely, we were deceived.

So let's see who's losing the war today.
I've switched it on at the wall.
No, dammit, I'll try the other side
And see who's winning football.

Work hard at the Coalface Son, or You'll have to teach in a School

Long ago, when G.B. had a thriving coal industry, the male population of mining towns and villages had little option but to work in the pits from the time they left school. A few parents, however, diligently scrimped and saved to get at least one boy into higher education and from there to a teachers' training college. Thus fathers would advise their sons to "Work hard at your studies, son, or you'll have to spend your life in the dust and gloom of the coalface."

This light hearted parody was written during my first year of teaching in a newly-formed inner-city comprehensive school. Teachers were literally dying or suffering serious stress-related illnesses or, in one case, getting stabbed with a chisel so, after four years and a messy divorce, while I was still reasonably sound in body and mind, I moved on, as you will see by other poems in this book.

1.

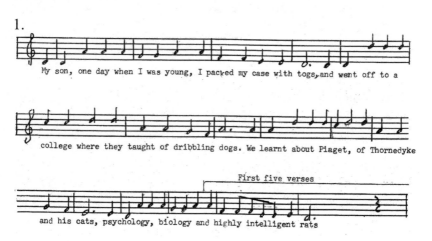

My son, one day when I was young, I packed my case with togs and went off to a college where they taught of dribbling dogs. We learnt about Piaget, of Thornedyke and his cats, psychology, biology and highly intelligent rats

First five verses

2.
I answered an advertisement
To teach inside a school,
And soon began to realise
I'd been a perfect fool.
The kids, they had no pens, to write
And few desired to work,
So thus they left me standing there,
A complete and utter burk.

3.
The headmaster was rarely seen,
The deputy was Hitler.
She made departmental heads feel small,
And me feel even littler.
She said, "You keep those kids so quiet
That I can hear no sounds."
Just then I wished that I could change
With Pavlov's dribbling hounds.

4.
At coffee-time, the staffroom filled
With tired and weary staff
Who commiserated with me.
Some even forced a laugh.
They said, "You'll get long holidays
For basking in the sun,
But I didn't have much appetite
For my sticky, currant bun.

5.
My name was on the notice-board
To do a duty at break.
I braved arctic conditions till
My bones began to ache.
A football hit me on the head.
It made me reel and spin.
My son, I hope you're listening!
I hope these words go in.

6.
My son, look at the spectacle
That stands before your eyes.
Your dad has been so foolish
But son, you must be wise.
Just take a tip from me, my lad,
And learn the golden rule.
You must work hard at the coalface, son,
or you'll have to teach in a school.

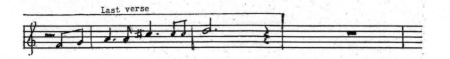

A Town without a Soul

Where are the streets we used to play in,
The bridge, we sheltered from the rain,
The trees we climbed, with nails to guide,
The coal trucks where we stole a ride,
The fields, we stalked each others' blood,
The stream, we jumped it, if we could,
The dark lanes where we spied on lovers,
Canal and railway up above us?
What have they done to my town?
What have they done to my town?

They sat and talked in a conference place,
Said, "This town needs a brand new face,
Plenty of work for heavy machines
And labourers clad in faded jeans."
They brought in experts to make a plan,
A town to suit the modern man,
A town to be famous from pole to pole,
But alas, a town without a soul.

Build it higher, higher, higher;
Unseen heat replaces fire.
Where to house the population?
If the lift breaks – isolation.
Next-door-neighbour is a stranger.
Where can kids play out of danger?
Graffiti covering the walls,
Obscene words and shameless scrawls.
What have they done to my town?
What have they done to my town?

A motorway runs past the doors.
It rattles windows, shakes the floors.

It fills the air with poison gas.
It shatters nerves as things whizz past.
The corner shop has lost the race,
A supermarket in its place,
Nameless girls in nylon coats,
A trolley full or a box of oats.
That's what they've done to my town!
That's what they've done to my town!

In thirty years it will turn out
They've built a slum, there is no doubt.
The high-rise flats will be pulled down.
So much for our new super town.
A generation on we'll see
Another plan for you and me,
A place where children love to play
But not for me, I'm on my way.

Old Canal Boat Rap   (Read lively)

Let's go, let's go to a place we know, chug.
Grass is green and the daisies grow, chug.
Water's still and the boats go slow, chug.
On the canal let's go, let's go. With a
Chug, chug, chug, chug, chug, chug, plut, chug,
Steering the boat along the cut, chug,
Ducking your head to miss the branches,
Steering with care, not taking chances,
Dodging a line with a float a-floating,
Keeping a watch for passing boating,
Watching a heron jump and fly fast,
Landing again in search of breakfast,
Kingfishers, voles and drakes and ducks, chug,
Listening to the engine, chug, chug, plut, chug.
Chug, chug, plut, chug.Chug, chug, plut, chug.
Listen to the engine, chug, chug, plut, chug.

Albert the Brummie's Son

Now Albert was a Brummie's Son
Who lived in AcocksGreen.
He drove a yellow Robin
With the front wheel in-between.

On Saturdays he took his tribe
To Lickey Hills or Clent,
But in the week he went to work
So as to pay the rent.

One day the car firm where he worked
Went into liquidation.
They said it was a general thing
Affecting all the nation.

So Albert thought he'd try his hand
At cleaning people's panes,
And now his car is Japanese
And he lives near Norton Canes.

Mother Shipton, Nostradamus; two of a group accredited with giving remarkably accurate forecasts about life in the future. Are their talents connected with information conferred from mysterious sources or do they, like science-fiction writers, cleverly build on possible outcomes of present situations? Here is a little food for thought.

Of Future Things

Of future things I am no seer
But here's one for a glass of beer.
Folks will eat meat that's grown in labs;
The slaughter-house will be for grabs.

A new ensign will be unfurled,
A super race will rule the world,
Their DNA so modified,
In games, in war, be on their side.

Of speed, there will be quite new limits,
Around the world in eighty minutes,
In vacuum tubes, deep underground,
Ballistic modules make no sound.

But time-travel, I doubt will be,
Just maybe, but it's fantasy.
"I've travelled back in time." he'll boast.
Folks of our time think he's a ghost.

A grand theory the new obsession
To dominate each science lesson;
The sun's a nucleus. My, that's cool!
The Milky Way's a molecule.

Atoms too small for observation
Could be home to civilization,
Universes, large and small,
Observed from our electron ball.

One thing to know, not least but last,
The future's built upon the past.
What we do now may repercuss.
What will the future blame on us?

The Anglia Hotel

It stood outside a second-hand shop in Chinhoyi, Zimbabwe, in remarkably good bodily condition considering it was nearly twenty years old. There was a good reason for this, - the climate. Nothing rusts out there. If it's made of steel it will seemingly last forever. Unlike wood, anything made of wood will be converted into dust by termites in a short time. This was why our house had steel doors, steel frames, steel skirting boards and a steel roof.

Anyway, the subject in question was a 1964 Ford Anglia 105E. We were in Zimbabwe on a three year contract to teach English. School holidays being generous, we decided to take full advantage of this once-in-a-lifetime opportunity to see as much of Africa, south of the Equator, as we could and, with a little modification, this vehicle would provide us with both transport and accommodation.

Nuts and bolts that would have to be ground out in this country were free to move easily each night as we converted the car into a camper, taking out the seats, using the rear ones to fill up the 'well' to make a reasonably flat platform on which to lie. Mosquito nets were fitted to the windows and, hey presto, we were the proud owners of the Anglia Hotel. In this way we travelled extensively through South Africa, Zambia, Tanzania, Malawi and, of course, Zimbabwe.

It seems odd that, in spite of a voluptuous amount of input, no poetry came out of these three years. Maybe it was because, during that time, my heart and mind were in tune with the world around me, my emotions were at peace. There is nothing like the cold steel of adversity to awaken dormant passions and challenge the writer to give expression to his innermost thoughts.

Mugs at Sixty-eight

The word spread through the feline world,
   'There's mugs at sixty-eight.
You only have to look half-starved;
   They'll feed you on a plate.

There's Kattavite and all the brands
   Well-advertised on telly.
No ginger tom nor Persian pet
   Should nurse an empty belly.'

So every mog in moggyland
   Turned up to grab his portion;
Some even seized their chance to make
   A bob, by shear extortion.

You've heard of eighteen-forty-nine
   When men rushed out for riches.
That's nothing to the scramble that
   Ensued in lanes and ditches.

One day, a sign was set up,
   On a post beside the gate,
The gist of which, translated, meant
   'No mugs at sixty-eight.'

As if that wasn't bad enough
   For every living mog,
The garden was soon occupied
   By an enormous dog.

What are you thinking?

What are you thinking as you crawl
Across my busy hand?
You walk across a poem
That you do not understand.

A little brain, a little life,
A 'Me,'' that's what you are,
Six legs and two antennae
And a body, black as tar.

You're capable of living and
Of eating to survive;
You'll reproduce your own and then
The species will all thrive.

Could I get in that brain of yours
To see what makes you tick?
They say it's just instinctive
But I think they must be thick.

We share this planet, you and I,
Live in the same location,
And yet a total barrier
Prevents communication.

So, off you go, to meet your own,
Perhaps they comprehend you,
For no prevailing power have I,
Whatever, to befriend you.

On the Zambezi

He was a young Rhodesian, typical of his kind – rich daddy, spoilt rotten, but generous and amiable to his Aryan genus.

The powerful outboard motor had been fixed to the transom of his speedboat by his African servant who had 'mistakenly' crossed the control cables. Thus, to turn right (or should I say starboard?), you turned the wheel to the left, and vice versa. It reminded me of a home-made trolley, or 'moke' I had as a boy which had the same design fault. I got used to it but, when a rival gang purloined it and took it as the spoils of war, they soon came a cropper, thus I got it back.

We set out at breakneck speed along the river until we came to a group of hippos happily paddling about on a submerged sandbank, a photo opportunity not to be missed. Unfortunately, as we approached, our guide forgot about the mismatched steering cables and, in an attempt to bring us, at a safe distance, broadside on to the group, swung the wheel the wrong way and beached us on the sandbank, surrounded by a family of hippopotami, non too pleased about this unwelcome intrusion into their peaceful activities. Now these beasts, despite their equable appearance have the reputation for being among the most dangerous four-footed animals in Africa. They have been known to smash boats and destroy all the occupants. Fortunately, on this occasion, they appeared to be in quite an amicable mood and merely showed an inquisitive interest as our escort, fortified with a little alcohol, stepped out of the boat and pushed it into deeper water.

Later that afternoon our cicerone returned with his pickup and offered to take us on a safari trip to look for lions. After a few miles in the bush the track was blocked by a bull elephant who, unlike the hippos, was not in a friendly mood. He stood on his hind legs, bellowed and made a mock charge. These highly intelligent creatures seem to know the difference between a mortal threat and mere interference so, in the latter case, a mock charge usually solves the problem without incurring retribution. I have never travelled so fast or so far in reverse gear. We were thankful that nobody had re-arranged the steering of the pickup.

Jools and the Professor's Chair

He's here again, that man named Jools,
A breaker of established rules.
He's now promoted – now Professor,
Of a chair, a proud possessor.

Thought it quite a good idea,
If his chair had voice and ear,
He could hold a conversation,
Put to rights wrongs of the nation,

Comment on the awful weather,
Oh! How nice to talk together,
Gossip all the latest scandal,
Stir the mud up with a handle.

"Mrs Jones has now got seven."
"Hubby's in the First Eleven."
"How can they afford such nice cars
While he's propping up the pub bars?"

But that's enough of idle chit-chat;
Not to mention Steven's tom-cat.
Let's get back to serious chatter;
These are things that really matter.

Jools's chair is made of hardwood;
Living, growing tree it once stood.
Sprouting leaves in reg'lar phases;
Hiding lovers from folks' gazes.

Once it had a life, that's true,
So Jools decided what to do.
He'd paint the chair with DNA
Ignoring what the critics say.

He'd modify its living genes,
Though we might not know what that means.
He'd mess around with chromosomes
And introduce some ziggyzones.

A double helix, so they say,
Is what you'll find in DNA
So to the breaker's yard he went
And bought two springs that weren't too bent.

He screwed them to the chair so neatly
They were out of sight completely.
If there was some verve left it
It should spring to life next minute.

Well, at last, the chair he sat on
Was a most unusual pattern.
Now a garrulous interlectual,
Talking sense, and so effectual.

Jools sat down with satisfaction,
Waiting for some interaction,
Found his chair not just a talker –
Genes had got in from a walker.

Up it got and started strolling,
Slow at first but then got rolling,
Out the lab and down the stairway,
In the street, across the fairway.

Shouts of 'fore' came from the golfers,
Laughter from the folk on sofas
Lounging under cosy sunshades,
Such excitement rare as mermaids.

But in front was e'en more import
As the chair approached an airport,
Sprouting wings, began to take off.
Too late now for Jools to jump off.

Up it soared to heights ethereal,
Reaching up to skies empyreal,
Past the cumulus, the nimbo,
Taking Jools, his arms akimbo.

═══════════

Now, another year was dawning.
All his friends were dressed in mourning.
Jools was lost; there was no doubting.
Life went on below without him.

Suddenly, quite unexpected,
'Twixt the converse interjected
Came a voice that was well-known.
Jools was on the telephone!

Such a tale he then recounted
Of the time he had spent mounted
On the chair of his invention
Loaded with such unconvention.

Jools and chair had been to China,
After that to Asia Minor,
Past the coast of Costa Brava,
Through the town of Bratislava,

On to Egypt, up the Nile,
Fought a hungry crocodile,
Caught it by the tail-hind-quarters,
Flung it back into the waters,

Circled round the Bell Rock Lighthouse,
In the States they saw the White House,
Great White sharks they watched in plenty,
Counted more than one-and-twenty,

Skimmed the top of Table Mountain,
Threw a coin in Trevi Fountain,
Climbed the Leaning Tower of Pisa,
Did all this without a visa!

By this time Jools wanted feeding
And the chair was also needing
Sustenance to keep it happy
So they found a transport café.

Off again, this time down under,
Threw a boomerang asunder
But it turned and came back to them,
Broke Chair's legs; no one could glue them!

PityJools – adventure finished!
But, with fervour undiminished,
Found his way back home next morning,
New ideas already dawning.

Loss Leader

Why can't we have simple prices?
Ev'ry shopping day's a crisis.
Two for one; this week it's butter.
Next week I'll beg, in the gutter!
Keep the coupon, when I choose it,
Fifty pence, if I don't lose it.
Win a house, a car, a phone.
Why can't they leave me alone?
Shall I buy a piece of steak?
Can't! It's doubled since last week!
Need a mind like a computer.
Who's idea? I think I'll shoot her.
At the checkout 'Have you got a
Card for points?' (I wish I'd shot her!)

Malawi

The Zomba Plateau owes its origin to forces beyond our imagination, as plate movements pushed and pulled as they attempted, unsuccessfully, to tear apart the continent that we now call Africa. Standing about three thousand feet above the surrounding land, the plateau could well have provided the inspiration for Sir Arthur Conan Doyle's 'The Lost World'. Sheer-sided with very little scree, it must have been almost inaccessible until someone carved two precarious narrow roads, one up and one down, inclined into its vertical walls.

The Anglia Hotel painstakingly ground its way up to the welcome cool climate and to the campsite with its amazingly modern aspect. Evergreen conifers grew in abundance and birds, familiar to the U.K., fluttered about in their branches. Walking here felt like it did at home, as long as you kept away from the edge. One false move would give you plenty of time for regret before you landed.

Before we set off for Malawi, someone in our school had told us of his uncle, who was captain of a ferry boat which regularly plied its way around the lake providing communications, supplies and trade to numerous villages on route, so we bought tickets for the round trip. There were no cabins or beds so the first night we spread our sleeping bags on the floor in the dining area only to find that, when darkness fell, we had the company of numerous cockroaches. I had learned previously, in the Sudan, that the best way to get rid of these repulsive creatures is to put a light on, a torch will do, and they will quickly disappear into their secret world. As we did not wish to spend the night shining torches at cockroaches we shook out our sleeping bags and took up our nocturnal residence on the table tops, thus our routine was established for the next few nights.

We arrived at one port of call at about seven o'clock in the evening, after dark. The village was a short walk along a well-defined track. After walking a little way, we became aware that there were things crawling about on the ground. Torches on, we saw them, scorpions, hundreds of them. Now, here's a tip; if you get off a boat on Lake Malawi after dark, wear your boots! We were wearing open sandals. Very carefully, we made a one-hundred-and-eighty-degree turn and picked our way back to the boat, fortunately unscathed.

Walking up another mountain in Malawi, I passed a man coming down in the opposite direction carrying a plank, not the most familiar sight on a mountain. A short while later, there was another, and then another, at intervals of perhaps twenty minutes. Each 'plankateer' was scantily clad and barefooted. Suddenly, a man stumbled and fell forward onto the rugged ground, his plank hurtling like a missile, down the steep incline in front of him. His toenail was almost severed. With some basic first-aid equipment I treated and bandaged his painful toe, then came the task of lifting the plank back onto his shoulder.

I had not noticed just how massive these planks were. I was a fairly fit fifty-year-old, toughened by the kind of activities in which I was currently engaged, and he was a man I wouldn't like to face in a boxing ring. (Not that I would have liked to face anyone in a boxing ring, having never been enamoured by that kind of sport), but it took all our combined effort to raise one end of the plank enough for him to get to a point of balance and swing the other end up off the ground. Thus he and his colleagues earnt, I was later told, £1-50 per day.

Further up the mountain I came to the source of those planks. A pit had been dug and a tree-trunk was stretched along the top. One man below and one man above were sawing along the trunk with a two-handled rip-saw. I felt ashamed that, at that very time, workers at home were bringing the economy to its knees by demanding more money and softer working conditions.

Footplate Fantasy

When I was a tot of tender years
I was taken to Snow Hill Station.
I stood with awe
At what I saw:
The mighty engines full of steam,
The first glimpse of my life-long dream,
And decided on my vocation.

The years went by, I reached thirteen
And gathered with others like-minded.
At Tamworth's 'low'
We watched them go,
'Peg on the clangers'* someone yells.
We hear the 'ding' of signalling bells,
To other sights we're blinded.

But one year on my head was turned
In quite a new direction.
I lost my way,
So as to say,
But, at the time, it seemed quite right
To put my childhood dreams to flight
And suffer their rejection.

When I look back (I'm now retired)
I'm often found regretting
I did not choose
To win or lose
Upon the footplate, by the fire,
And thus fulfil my heart's desire.
But what's the use of fretting?

* Signals at Tamworth that used to bounce with a clanging
sound when returning to the horizontal position.

Wrekin' Havoc

There once was a man on the air
Who bought a delightful young mare.
One day, up the Wrekin,*
The horse started speakin'
So now they broadcast as a pair.

* The Wrekin is a notable Shropshire Hill, rising from a level plain. It has given rise to the saying, 'going all round the Wrekin', referring to a long-winded explanation.

The Ballad of the Burnt-out Clutch

I once set out for the Stretton hills
On an ancient bike and chair, *
With a wife and babe, two teenage girls,
A kitten (or a pup) and lots of sup,
For a day in the clean, fresh air.

Returning over Wenlock Edge
A thunder storm we saw.
It was not too near so we had no fear.
The lightning struck like an angry buck
And we heard the thunder roar.

We made our way to Wenlock town
But on the Bridgnorth road
The clutch burnt out, the storm caught up,
The street lamps failed, the rain came down
And the wind just blowed and blowed.

We moved into a B & B
And dried our soggy gear,
With a wife and babe, two teenage girls,
A kitten (or a pup) but very little sup.
In the morning, the sky was clear.

I took the bus to Wellington
Through a most enchanting view,
The Ironbridge Gorge, the ancient bridge;
I got the plates and fixed the bike,
Then knew what I must do.

We sold our house in Birmingham
And moved out Ironbridge way,
And many the years, some dressed with tears,
Have passed between the changing scene
But we're still there to this day.
* sidecar

The Banana Express

The campsite at Port Elizabeth overlooks a bay in the Indian Ocean. A triangular dorsal fin, so massive that at first we took it for a small black sail, darted across the bay, followed by another smaller one. Did they both belong to the same animal or were there two? Was it a Great White? We think so.

A puffing sound drew our attention to the landward side of the site, sweet music to a railway enthusiast's ears. Sure enough, a small engine, followed by a number of goods waggons, was making its laborious way up the steady incline that, hitherto unobserved, bordered the camp site. This was a bonus!

Travelling without a guide book has its compensations. Maps are essential to travel but guide books take away the surprise element, they tell you what to expect, fill you with excitement and then, human nature being what it is, sometimes disappoint you. I remember while cycling around Lake Maggiore, after passing from Italy across the Swiss border, hearing the sweet sound of barrel organs playing by the lakeside. (One of the best things about cycling or walking is that you hear things before you see them.) The sight that met my eyes, combined with the sound of the instruments, brought spontaneous delight to the senses.

Let's get back to the Banana Express. It is a double misnomer, there are no bananas and, as the narrow-guage loco winds its burdensome way up into the mountains of Zulu country, it can hardly be called an express. Is that another train going the other way? No! It's the front end of the Banana Express passing us in the opposite direction as it negotiates one of the many hairpin bends on route.

The train transports timber from its source down to the docks at Port Elizabeth. For the benefit of railway 'cranks' like the writer, and for the more adventurous of tourists, a small observation car is coupled to the rear, consisting of one compartment with bench seats facing front and back. At that time the apartheid system was in full force. Toilets were marked black men, white men, black ladies and white ladies. We had once come across a poster depicting a youthful Nelson Mandela with the caption 'Free this Man'. The carriage in which we sat did not need to be marked, all knew it was for whites. This was why, on the return journey, we saw a man pick up a large stone and throw it with great force at the carriage. It broke the thick glass of the window, travelled across the empty seat opposite us and hit the other window before dropping onto the seat. A short while before, the seat had been occupied by a family with a boy of about ten years of age who sat by the window that was now shattered. Mercifully they had left the train a short while before. When the opportunity arose I told the driver who shrugged resignedly and said it often happened.

"Remember now thy Creator in the days of thy youth"
Ecclesiastes 12:1

The River of Life

Part 1.
The Youth   (Part 1 of this poem was written in 1952, Part 2,
                   fifty-eight years later.)

I dreamed I was an old man
Full of years and sad remorse
That my life had been so fruitless
When it could have been a force.
I gazed upon those trembling hands
Through eyes so weak and dim,
It seemed my Lord was asking me
What had they done for Him?

Those feet had trodden many a land
From icy waste to tropic,
Those lips now slurred and marred by age
Once spoke of many a topic.
And yet it seemed I failed to use
These faculties God-given
To publish forth the word of life
And show the way to Heaven.

What could the future hold for me?
Could I now start and learn
God's Word with mind and memory dull?
Could I now make a turn?
Alas my years are nearly through,
They cannot be retrieved.
Regret is written in my heart
And sorrow is conceived.

I slowly left the world of sleep
To consciousness awoke,
A ray of light had pierced my room
The birds their language spoke.
The air was filled with freshness and
A new day had begun.
It scarce seemed true that I was young,
Fresh as the morning sun.

A song of joy which filled my heart
Surpassed the sparrows' song
To work for God was my desire,
To serve Him well and long.
The years stretched out before me
Like a field of ripened corn.
The truth had gripped and thrilled my soul
For life was in its morn.

Could I now waste these coming years
With talents given free?
Could feet and hands and eyes and mouth
Now be used selfishly?
Nay, while I've breath and health and time
My Lord shall have the best
Until he calls me, satisfied,
To my eternal rest.

Part 2

The Old Man

And now I am an old man
Full of years but not remorse.
In my youth I knew the answers:
Just the questions stayed the course
Of the long and changeful river

That impels my humble craft
From the unison of streamlets
In the mountains now far aft.

Past the early years, awakening
To the earth's vast treasure store.
Past light and shade and hill and glade,
Past strange desires, and more.

Through youthful, tum-ber-ling cascades,
Through mosses soft and damp,
Past stepping-stones and bridges
Where the outdoor-lovers camp,

Past meadows that are fringed with gorse,
Past mills that grind the grain,
Their mighty wheels a-groaning
As they tussle with the strain
Like men who earn their daily bread
By toil and sweat and pain
Regardless of the consequence
Of working in the rain.

That river now impels my craft
Through waters calm and free
As it flows, now slightly salty,
Ambling on towards the sea.

Far behind, the tumbling rapids
Where the whitest waters foam
Like a dove without a cote,
Like a man without a home
There I drifted in my solitude
Through gorges dark and drear.
My small pontoon was near destroyed,
My end, it seemed was near.

"Not yet! Not yet!" a voice rang out,
"You must needs reach the sea."
You may yet see a delta
Or an island or levee."

I spy the gulls on soaring wings;
I hear their plaintive cry.
The sky before is waxing bright;
No high land do I spy.
Methinks it won't be very long
Before I reach the sea.
Perhaps the answer to my quest
Is waiting there for me.

Twilight Journey

With my head upon my pillow,
Just before I go to sleep,
There's a land I travel into.
Would you like to take a peep?

There are time-flies making minutes.
Brick-bats fly across the House.
I just saw one hit the Commons cat
Who thought it was a mouse.

There, the Whys Owl asks the questions
While the May Bee is in doubt
And the wheelybug does clever stunts
Each time they let him out.

At the Bokowonko tournament
They hail the latest winner
As crow-flies make their beelines
While the felines are at dinner.

Now, the Thief of Time is on the loose;
The time-flies don't want hassle
So they fly indoors before he takes
One off into his castle.

Teledactyls stare on straight ahead,
Not noticing I'm there,
So I sing and shout and dance about
But still they do not care.

Then at last I reach the old canal
And climb aboard my boat.
In a cosy little cabin
I shall spend the night afloat.

Good night!

Index to Poems

Index to Memoirs etc